Extraordinary Insects

Extraordinary Insects

Weird. Wonderful. Indispensable.
The Ones Who Run Our World.

Anne Sverdrup-Thygeson

Translation by Lucy Moffatt

MUDLARK

Mudlark
An imprint of HarperCollins*Publishers*
1 London Bridge Street
London SE1 9GF

www.harpercollins.co.uk

First published by J.M. Stenersens Forlag AS 2018

This UK edition published by Mudlark 2019

1 3 5 7 9 10 8 6 4 2

Text © Anne Sverdrup-Thygeson 2018

Translation © Lucy Moffatt 2019

This translation has been published with the financial support of
NORLA, Norwegian Literature Abroad

Chapter illustrations © Tuva Sverdrup-Thygeson 2018

Illustrations on pages 21, 42, 68, 95, 122, 144,
176, 233 © Carim Nahaboo 2019

Anne Sverdrup-Thygeson asserts the moral right
to be identified as the author of this work

A catalogue record of this book is available from
the British Library

HB ISBN 978-0-00-831635-8
TPB ISBN 978-0-00-831636-5

Printed and bound in Great Britain by
CPI Group (UK) Ltd, Croydon, CR0 4YY

MIX
Paper from
responsible sources
FSC™ C007454

This book is produced from independently certified FSC paper
to ensure responsible forest management.

For more information visit: www.harpercollins.co.uk/green

Nature is nowhere as great as in its smallest creatures

PLINY THE ELDER

Naturalis historia 11, 1.4,

Ca. 79 CE

Contents

List of illustrations

Preface

I've always liked spending time outdoors, especially in the forest. Preferably in places where signs of human life are few and far between, and evidence of our modern impact scarce; among trees older than any living person, trees that have toppled headlong, nose-diving into the springy moss. Here they lie, in prostrate silence, as life continues its eternal round dance.

The insects come to the dead trees in their hordes. Bark beetles party in the sap that ferments beneath the bark, longhorn beetle larvae trace ingenious patterns on the surface of the wood, and like tiny crocodiles, wireworms greedily snap up anything that moves within the rotting wood. Together, thousands of insects, fungi and bacteria work to break down dead matter and transform it into new life.

I feel incredibly lucky to be able to research such an exciting topic, because I have a fantastic job: I am a professor at the Norwegian University of Life Sciences (NMBU), where I work as a scientist, teacher and communicator.

One day I might be reading about new research, digging deep and losing myself in scientific detail. The next, I'm due to give a lecture and have to look for an overarching structure in a given subject area, find examples and illustrate why the issue matters to you and me. Maybe it will end up as a post on our research blog, Insektøkologene (The Insect Ecologists).

Sometimes I work outdoors. I seek out ancient, hollow oaks or map forests affected to varying degrees by logging. All this I do in the company of my wonderful colleagues and students.

When I tell people I work with insects, they often ask me: What good are wasps? Or: Why do we even need mosquitoes and deer flies? Because some insects are a nuisance, of course. The truth is, though, that they are a vanishingly small minority compared with the teeming myriads of tiny critters that all do their little bit to save your life, every single day. But let's start with the more troublesome ones. I have three answers.

First of all, these annoying insects are useful to nature. Mosquitoes and gnats are vital food for fish, birds, bats and other creatures. In the highlands and the far north of Norway, in particular, swarms of flies and mosquitoes are crucial to animals much larger than themselves, and on a vast scale. During the short, hectic Arctic summer, insect swarms can determine where the large reindeer flocks graze, trample the earth and deposit nutrition in the form of dung. This has ripple effects that influence the whole ecosystem. Similarly, wasps are useful, both for us and other creatures. They help pollinate plants, gobble up pests whose numbers we'd rather keep down and provide food for honey buzzards and countless other species.

Secondly, helpful solutions may await us where we least expect them. This even applies to creatures we see as disgusting nuisances. For example, blow flies can cleanse hard-to-heal wounds, while mealworms turn out to be able to digest plastic, and scientists are currently investigating the use of cockroaches for rescue work in collapsed or severely polluted buildings, as we will see in Chapter 8.

Thirdly, many people think that all species should have the opportunity to achieve their full life potential – that we humans have no right to play fast and loose with species diversity driven by short-sighted judgements about which species we see as cute or useful. This means we have a moral duty to take the best possible care of our planet's myriad creatures – including critters that do not engage in any visible value creation, insects that do not have soft fur and big brown eyes and species we see no point in.

Nature is bewildering in its complexity and insects are a significant part of these ingeniously constructed systems in which we humans are just one species among millions of others. That is why this book will deal with the very smallest among us: all the strange, beautiful and bizarre insects underpinning the world as we know it.

The first part of the book is about the insects themselves. In Chapter 1, you can read about their mindbogglingly rich variety, how they are put together, how they sense their surroundings, and a bit about how to recognise the most important insect groups. Then in Chapter 2, you'll gain an insight into their rather strange sex lives. After that, I'll dig deeper into the intricate interplay between insects and other animals (Chapter 3), and between insects and plants (Chapter 4): the daily struggle to eat or be eaten in which every creature battles to pass on its own genes. Yet there is still room for collaboration, in countless peculiar ways.

The rest of the book is about insects' intimate relationship with one particular species: us humans. How they contribute to our food supply (Chapter 5), clean up the natural environment (Chapter 6) and give us some of the things we need, from honey to antibiotics (Chapter 7). In Chapter 8, I take a look at new fields where insects can lead the way. Finally, in Chapter 9, I consider how these tiny helpers of ours are getting along, and how you and I can help improve their lot. Because we humans rely on insects getting their job done. We need them for pollination, decomposition and soil formation; to serve as food for other animals, keep harmful organisms in check, disperse seeds, help us in our research and inspire us with their smart solutions. Insects are nature's little cogs that make the world go round.

Introduction

There are more than 200 million insects for every human being living on Planet Earth today. As you sit reading this sentence, between one and 10 trillion insects are shuffling and crawling and flapping around on the planet, outnumbering the grains of sand on all the world's beaches. Like it or not, they have you surrounded, because Earth is the planet of the insects.

There are so very many of them that it's difficult to take it in, and they are everywhere: in forests and lakes, meadows and rivers, tundra and mountains. Stoneflies live in the chilly heights of the Himalayas at altitudes of 6,000 metres, while mosquito larvae inhabit the piping-hot springs of Yellowstone, where temperatures exceed 50°C. In the eternal darkness of the world's deepest caverns live blind cave midges. Insects also live in baptismal fonts, computers, oil puddles, and in the acid and bile of a horse's stomach. They live in deserts, beneath the ice on frozen seas, in the snow and in the nostrils of walruses.

Insects live on all continents – although they are admittedly represented by only a single species on Antarctica: a flightless midge that kicks the bucket if the temperature happens to creep more than 10 degrees above zero for any length of time. There are even insects in the sea. Seals and penguins have various kinds of lice in their hides, which remain in place when their hosts dive beneath the surface. And we mustn't forget the louse that lives in a pelican's pouch, or the water striders who spend their lives scudding six-legged across the open sea. Insects may be tiny but their achievements are far from trifling.

Long before human beings set foot on this planet, insects had already taken up agriculture and animal husbandry: termites grow fungus for food, while ants keep aphids as dairy cattle. Wasps were the first creatures to make paper from cellulose and caddisfly larvae were catching other creatures in net-like webs millions of years before we humans managed to weave our first fishing nets. Insects solved complicated problems of aerodynamics and navigation several million years ago, and learnt, if not how to tame fire, then at least how to tame light – even within their own bodies.

Insects Assemble

Whether we opt to count them by individual or species, there are good grounds for claiming that insects are the most successful class of animal on the planet. Not only are there incredible numbers of individual insects, they also account for well over *half* of all known multicellular species. They come in around a million different variants. This means that you could have an 'insect of the month' calendar featuring a new species every single month for more than 80,000 years!

From A to Z, insects impress with their species richness: ants, bumblebees, cicadas, dragonflies, earwigs, fireflies, grasshoppers, honeybees, inchworms, jewel beetles, katydids, lacewings, mayflies, nits, owl moths, praying mantises, queen butterflies, rice weevils, stinkbugs, termites, urania moths, velvet ants, wasps, xylophagous beetles, yellow mealworms and zebra butterflies.

Let's do a quick thought experiment: to get an impression of how species diversity is distributed among different groups of species, imagine if all the world's known species – big and small alike – were given UN membership. It would be an awfully tight squeeze in the assembly chambers because even if there was only a single representative for every species, that would still add up to well over one and a half million representatives.

Let's say we distributed power and voting rights in this 'UN of biodiversity' according to the number of species in the different species groups. That would throw up new and unusual patterns, largely because insects would dominate, comprising more than half of all votes. And that's before we consider all the other small species, such as spiders, snails, roundworms and the like, which alone would account for a fifth of the votes. Next up, plant species of all kinds would total roughly 16 per cent, while known species of fungus and lichen would command around 5 per cent of votes.

But where do we fit into this picture? When we look at species diversity like this, humanity doesn't amount to much. Even if we were counted along with *all* the rest of the world's vertebrates – with animals like elk and mice, fish, birds, snakes and frogs – we would still end up with a minuscule share of power, constituting a mere 3 per cent of known species diversity. In other words, we humans are totally dependent on a host of tiny, anonymous species, a significant proportion of which are insects.

Dwarf Fairies and Biblical Giants

Insects come in all shapes and hues, spanning a range of sizes that is barely matched in any other class of animal. The world's tiniest insects, fairy wasps, live out the whole of their larval existence inside the eggs of other insects, which gives you a good idea of just how small they are. One of them, the teeny little *Kikiki huna* wasp, is so tiny at 0.16mm that you can't even see it. It takes its name from the official Polynesian language spoken on Hawaii, one of the places where it is found. Logically enough, it means something like 'tiny little dot'.

A sister species among the dwarf wasps has an even prettier name: *Tinkerbella nana* takes its genus name from the fairy in *Peter Pan*, while the species name 'nana' is a pun referring to both 'nanos', the Greek word for 'dwarf', and Nana, the name of the dog in *Peter Pan*. The Tinkerbell wasp is so small that it can land on the tip of a human hair.

It's a giant step from there to our biggest insects. There are several rivals for this title, depending on what you take 'biggest' to mean. If we're talking longest, then the winner is the Chinese stick insect *Phryganistria chinensis Zhao*: at 62.4cm, it is longer than your forearm. That said, it is no thicker than an index finger. The subspecies was named for entomologist Zhao Li, who spent six years of his life hunting down the super stick insect after a tip-off from locals in the Guangxi region of southern China.

But if we're talking about the heaviest insect, the goliath beetle is well placed. The larvae of this African giant can weigh up to 100g – roughly the same as a blackbird. The beetle was named after Goliath, the 10-foot giant of biblical fame who struck terror into the hearts of the Israelites but was nonetheless slain by a stripling called David, aided only by a sling – and a fair amount of help from friends in high places.

The Very First Insects Predate the Dinosaurs

Insects have been around for a long time, infinitely longer than us humans. It's difficult to get a proper grasp on deep time: aeons and eras, millions and billions of years. So perhaps it won't mean all that much if I say that the first insects saw the light of day around 479 million years ago. Maybe it's more helpful to point out that insects saw the dinosaurs both come and go, by a long margin.

Once upon a time, long, long ago, the first plants and animals emerged from the sea and onto dry land. It was a revolution for life on Earth. Imagine if we could have filmed this fateful moment – what an iconic video clip that would be: 'One small step for bugs, one giant leap for life on Earth.' Unfortunately, we'll have to settle for tracking the entrepreneurs of the insect world using fossils and our own fertile imagination.

Think back to the Earth's earliest days. A few million years have passed since the first adventurous bugs poked their heads out of the sea and decided to check out new, drier neighbourhoods. We are in the Devonian period, somewhat anonymously sandwiched between two better-known eras, the Cambro-Silurian period (consisting of the Cambrian, Ordovician and Silurian – which gave rise to the limestone-rich areas around Oslo, Norway) and the Carboniferous period (part of the very basis for our fossil fuel dependent society, with all its attendant wealth and climate change). Evolution has shifted into top gear and the first insect is now a fact: down there on the ground amid the bracken and the plants shaped like crow's feet shuffles a tiny six-legged creature, with three body segments and two small antennae. It is the planet's first ever insect, taking the first small steps towards total world domination by its kind.

The close interaction between insects and other life forms was crucial from their very first day on dry land. Land plants improved the life chances of insects and other bugs by providing them with sustenance up there on the stony, barren earth. In return, the bugs improved the plants' life chances by recycling the nutrition in dead plant tissue and creating soil for new growth.

The Wonder of Wings

One important reason for insects' enormous success is that they can fly. What a fantastic innovation that must have been, around 400 million years ago! Now insects had access to something totally unique: equipped with wings, they could reach the nutrition up in the plants more efficiently while simultaneously avoiding earthbound enemies. For the more adventurous, wings offered brand new opportunities to disperse to pastures new. Access to airspace also influenced choice of partner, giving insects undreamed-of opportunities to flaunt their best features in new, sky-high pick-up joints.

We don't know exactly when wings first developed. Perhaps they evolved from outgrowths on the thoracic area; outgrowths that may have served as solar collectors or a means of stabilising the body after a jump or a fall. Perhaps the wings evolved from gills. Regardless, the most important point here is that insects discovered that these gadgets of theirs were also brilliant for gliding down from trees or high plants. Insects with well-developed wing nubs got more food, lived longer and – as a result – had more offspring, which, in turn, inherited these super wing nubs. In this way, evolution ensured that wings became commonplace, and at a pretty rapid rate, too, in the context of geological timescales. Soon the air was alive with all manner of shimmering, whirring wings.

One point is crucial to understanding how wildly successful wings were for the early insects: *nobody else* could fly! There were not yet any birds, bats or pterosaurs, and they would be a long time coming. This meant that insects had global dominance of the air for more than 150 million years. In comparison, our own species, *Homo sapiens*, has spent a total of just 200,000 short years on the planet.

Insects have survived five rounds of mass extinction. The dinosaurs first staggered out into the world after the third of these, around 240 million years ago. So next time you catch yourself thinking how irritating an insect is, bear in mind that this animal class has been on the planet since long before the dinosaurs. That alone merits a little respect, if you ask me.

CHAPTER 1

Small Creatures, Smart Design:
Insect Anatomy

S o how are they put together, these tiny creatures with whom we share our planet? The following section is a crash course in insect construction. It also shows that, despite their modest size, insects can count, teach and recognise both each other and us humans.

Six Legs, Four Wings, Two Antennae

What exactly is an insect? If you're in any doubt, a good rule of thumb is to start by counting legs. Because most insects have six legs, all attached to the mid-section of their body.

The next step is to check whether the bug has wings. These are also on the mid-section. Most insects have two pairs of wings: forewings and hindwings.

You have now indirectly grasped one crucial hallmark of

insects: their bodies are divided into three. As one of many representatives of the phylum Arthropoda, insects are formed of many segments, although in their case, these have merged into three pretty clear and distinct sections: head, thorax and abdomen. The old segments still appear as indentations or marks on the surface of many insects, as if somebody had cut them with a sharp implement – and in fact, that is what gave this class of animal its name: the word 'insect' comes from the Latin verb 'insecare', meaning to cut into.

The front segment, the head, isn't so unlike our own: it has both a mouth and the most important sense organs – eyes and antennae. While insects never have more than two antennae, their eyes can vary in number and type. And just so you know: insects don't necessarily only have eyes on their head. One species of swallowtail butterfly has eyes on its penis! These help the male to position himself correctly during mating. The female also has eyes on her rear end, which she uses to check she is laying her eggs in the right place.

If the head is the insect's sensory centre, the mid-section – the thorax – is the transport centre. This segment is dominated by the muscles needed to power the wings and legs. It is worth noting that, unlike all other creatures that can fly or glide – birds, bats, flying squirrels, flying fish – insect wings are not repurposed arms or legs but separate motor devices that supplement the legs.

The abdomen, which is often the largest segment, is responsible for reproduction and also contains most of the insect's gut system. Gut waste is excreted at the rear – usually. The minute gall wasp larvae, which live out their larval existence in the completely closed structure the plant builds around them, are extremely well brought up. They know it's wrong to foul your own nest and since they are trapped in a one-room flat without a toilet, they have no choice but to hold it in. Only once the larval stage is complete are the gut and the gut opening connected. *See also Chapter 7, page 181.*

Living in an Invertebrate World

Insects are invertebrates – in other words, animals without a backbone, skeleton or bones. Instead, their skeleton is on the outside: a hard yet light exoskeleton protects the soft interior against collision and other external stresses. The outermost surface is covered in a layer of wax, which offers protection against every insect's greatest fear: dehydration. Despite their small size, insects have a large surface area relative to their tiny volume – meaning that they are at high risk of losing precious water molecules through evaporation, which would leave them as dead as dried fish. The wax layer is a crucial means of hanging onto every molecule of moisture.

The same material that forms the skeleton around the body also protects the legs and wings. The legs are strong, hollow tubes with a number of joints that enable the insect to run and jump and do other fun things.

But there are a few disadvantages to having your skeleton on the outside. How are you supposed to grow and expand if you're shut in like this? Imagine bread dough encased in medieval armour, expanding and rising until it has nowhere left to go. But insects have a solution: new armour, soft to start with, forms beneath the old. The old, rigid armour cracks open and the insect jumps out of its skin as casually as we'd shrug off a well-worn shirt. Now it's crucial for the insect to literally inflate itself to make the new, soft armour as big as possible before it dries and hardens. Because once the new exoskeleton has hardened, the insect's potential for growth is determined until another moulting paves the way for new opportunities.

If you think this sounds tiring, it may be a consolation to hear that (with a few exceptions) the lengthy moulting process only occurs in insects' early lives.

Time of Transformation

Insects come in two variants: those that change gradually through a series of moultings and those that undergo an abrupt change in the process of developing from child to adult. This transformation is called a metamorphosis.

The first type – e.g. dragonflies, grasshoppers, cock-roaches and true bugs (*see also page 36*) – gradually change in appearance as they grow. A bit like us humans, except that we don't have to shed our entire skin in order to flour-ish. For these insects, the childhood stage is known as the nymph stage. The nymphs grow, cast off their exoskeleton a few times (just how many times varies by species, but often three to eight times) and become increasingly like the adult versions. Then, finally, the nymph moults one last time and crawls out of its used larval skin equipped with functioning wings and sex organs: voilà! It has become an adult!

Other insects undergo a complete metamorphosis – an almost magical change in appearance from child to adult. In our human world, we have to turn to fairy tales and fantasy for examples of this sort of shapeshifting, like kissed frogs turning into princes, or J.K. Rowling's Professor Minerva McGonagall shapeshifting into a cat. But for insects, kiss-ing and spells aren't the cause of the change: the metamor-phosis is driven by hormones and marks the transition from child to adult. First, the egg hatches into a larva that looks nothing like the creature it will ultimately become. The larva often resembles a dull, pale rectangular bag, with a mouth at one end and an anus at the other (although there are honourable exceptions, including many butterflies). The larva moults several times, growing bigger on each occasion but otherwise looking pretty much unchanged.

The magic happens in the pupal stage – a period of rest in which the insect undergoes the miraculous change from anonymous 'bag creature' to an incredibly complicated, ingeniously constructed adult individual. Inside the pupal case, the whole insect is rebuilt, like a Lego model whose blocks are pulled apart and put back together again to make an entirely different shape. In the end, the pupa splits and out climbs 'a beautiful butterfly' – as described in one of my all-time favourite children's books, *The Very Hungry Caterpillar*. Total transformation is brilliant and undoubtedly the most successful variant. Most insect species on the planet, 85 per cent of them, undergo this type of complete metamorphosis. This includes the dominant insect groups, such as beetles, wasps, butterflies, flies and mosquitoes.

The ingenious part of it is that insects can exploit two totally different diets and habitats as child and adult, concentrating on their central task in each phase of their lives. The earthbound larvae, whose focal point is energy storage, can be eating machines. Then, in the pupal stage, all the accumulated energy is melted down and reinvested in a totally new organism: a flying creature dedicated to reproduction.

➤◉◄

The connection between larvae and adult insects has been known since Ancient Egyptian times, but people didn't understand what was happening. Some thought that the larva was a stray foetus that eventually came to its senses and crawled back into its egg – in the form of the pupa – in order to be born at last. Others claimed that two totally different individuals were involved, the first of which died and was then resurrected in a new form.

Only in the 1600s did Dutch biologist Jan Swammerdam with his new invention, the microscope, demonstrate that the larva and the adult insect were one and the same individual throughout. The microscope enabled people to see that if a larva or pupa was cut open carefully, clearly recognisable elements of the grown insect could be found beneath the surface. Swammerdam enjoyed displaying his skills with scalpel and microscope before an audience, and used to demonstrate how he could remove the skin from a big silkworm larva to reveal the wing structure beneath, complete with the characteristic veined patterning on the wings. Even so, this did not become general knowledge until much, much later. In his journal, Charles Darwin notes that a German scientist was charged with heresy in Chile as late as the 1830s because he could transform larvae into butterflies. Experts continue discussing the exact details of the metamorphosis process even now. Luckily, there are still some mysteries left in this world.

Breathing Through a Drinking Straw

Insects don't have lungs and don't breathe through their mouths like we do. Instead, they breathe through holes in the sides of their bodies. The holes run, like drinking straws, from the surface of the insect into its interior, branching out along the way. Air fills the straws and the oxygen then passes out of them and into the body's cells. This means that insects don't need to use their blood to transport oxygen to the various nooks and crannies of their bodies. However, they do still need some kind of blood – known as haemolymph – to carry nutrition and hormones to the cells and to clear them of waste material. Since insect blood doesn't transport oxygen, there is no need for the ferrous red substance that colours our mammal blood red. Consequently, insect blood is colourless, yellow or green. That is why your car windscreen doesn't end up looking like a scene from a bad crime novel when you're driving along on a hot, still, summer afternoon but is instead covered in yellowish-green splatters.

Insects don't even have veins and arteries: instead, insect blood sloshes around freely among the bodily organs, down into the legs and out into the wings. To ensure a bit of circulation, there is a heart of sorts: a long dorsal tube with muscles, and openings on the side and at the front. Muscle contractions pump the blood forward from the rear, towards the head and the brain.

Insects' sensory impressions are processed in the brain. It is tremendously important for them to pick up signals from their surroundings in the form of scent, sound and sight if they are to find food, avoid enemies and pick up partners. Although insects have the same basic senses as us humans – they sense light, sound and smell, and can taste and feel – most of their sense organs are constructed in a totally different way. Let's take a look at insects' sensory apparatus.

The Fragrant Language of Insects

The sense of smell is important for many insects, although, unlike us, they lack a nose, doing most of their smelling through their antennae instead. Some insects, including certain male butterflies, have large feathery antennae that can pick up the scent of a female several kilometres away, even in extremely low concentrations.

In many ways, insects communicate through smell. Scent molecules allow them to send each other various kinds of messages, from personal ads such as 'Lonesome lady seeks handsome fella for good times' to ant restaurant recommendations: 'Follow this scent trail to a delicious dollop of jam on the kitchen counter.'

Spruce bark beetles, for example, don't need Snapchat or Messenger to tell each other where the party is. When they discover an ailing spruce tree, they shout about it in the language of scent. This enables them to gather together enough beetles to overpower a sickly, living tree – which ends its days as a kindergarten for thousands of beetle babies.

We miss out on most of these insect scents, which we simply can't smell. But if you wander beneath the greenery of ancient trees on a late summer's day in the town of Tønsberg, southern Norway, you may be lucky enough to pick up the most delightful aroma of peaches: it is the hermit beetle, one of Europe's largest and rarest beetles, wooing a girlfriend in the neighbouring tree. The substance it uses rejoices in the thoroughly unromantic name of gamma-Decalactone and we humans produce it in labs for use in cosmetics, and to add aroma to food and drink.

The scent is very helpful to the hermit beetle, which is heavy and sluggish and seldom flies, or not far at any rate. It lives in ancient, hollow trees, where its larvae gnaw on rotted wood debris, and it's a real homebody: a Swedish study found that most adult hermit beetles were still living in the same tree they were born in. This lack of interest in travel complicates the business of finding new hollow trees to move into, and the situation is hardly helped by the fact that old, hollow trees are an unusual phenomenon in today's intensively exploited forest and farmland.

As a result, the species, which is scattered across Western Europe, from southern Sweden to northern Spain (though not the British Isles), is decreasing all over its range and is protected in many European countries. In Norway, it is considered critically endangered and can be found in only one place: an old churchyard in Tønsberg. Or *two* places to be precise, because some individuals have recently been moved to a nearby oak grove in an effort to secure the survival of the species.

Flowery Temptresses

Flowers have realised that scent is important to insects. Or rather, millions of years of mutual evolution have resulted in the most incredible interactions. The world's largest flower, which belongs to the *Rafflesia* genus and is found in Southeast Asia, is pollinated by blow flies. This means that 'a scent of warm summer sun meets a cool evening breeze with a hint of amber and sensual vanilla' – to borrow perfume industry terminology – isn't going to cut the mustard. No indeed! If you want blow flies to come visiting, you need to yell at them in blow-fly language. That is why the world's biggest flower smells like a dead animal whose carcass has been lying around in the heat of the jungle a couple of days too many – a stench of rotting flesh that is utterly irresistible if you happen to be a blow fly.

But you don't have to visit the jungle to find examples of flowers that speak the insects' language of scent. The fly orchid is a protected native European species, rare in Norway and the UK, but widespread throughout central Europe. It has strange brownish-blue flowers that look just like the female of a certain digger wasp species and its beautiful appearance is supplemented by the right scent: the flower smells identical to a female digger wasp on the pull. So, what is a bewildered newly hatched male digger wasp to do, whose short life is dominated by but a single thought? He falls for the trick and tries to mate with the flower. When things don't go so well, he moves on to what he thinks is the next female and tries again. No luck there, either. But what he doesn't know is that during these ill-fated pairings, he has picked up some yellow structures that look a bit like 'deely-boppers' – popular party headwear if you remember the Eighties. These structures contain the fly orchid's pollen, so the male digger wasp's feverish flirting contributes to the flowers' pollination.

And if you're concerned about the fate of the unfortunate male, please don't despair. The real females hatch a few days after the males and then things really start hotting up. In this way, the existence of both the fly orchid and the digger wasp is assured.

Eyes on their Knees and Deathwatch Beetles

Although communicating through scent is important for insects, especially when searching for a mate, some rely on sound to find a partner instead. The grasshopper's song is not designed to create the sound of summer for us humans, but to find a girlfriend for this little green critter. Because it is usually the male calling out to the female, in the same way as male birds are frequently the keenest warblers. If you've heard the deafening wall of sound cicadas create in southern climes, bear in mind that it would be twice as loud if the females joined in, but as an Ancient Greek saying has it: 'Blessed are the cicadas for they have voiceless wives.' Controversial as we may find this statement in modern society, let me just add that it may be pretty smart of the females to keep their lips zipped. Lovesick fellow cicadas aren't the only ones attracted by the song: scary parasites lie in wait, listening, then sneak up to lay a tiny little egg on the soloist. And although it might look quite innocent, it's game over for the singer. The egg hatches into a hungry larva, which consumes the cicada from the inside out. Enough said.

Insects have ears in all sorts of peculiar places but rarely on their heads. They may be on their legs, their wings, their thorax or their abdomen. Certain butterflies even have ears in their mouths! Insect ears come in a number of variants and even though all of them are XXXS size, some are incredibly intricate. One type has a vibrating membrane, like a tiny drum, whose skin is set in motion every time sound waves from the air reach it. It isn't so unlike our own inner ear, just in a simplified miniature version.

Insects can also sense sound through different sensors connected to small hairs which pick up vibrations. Mosquitoes and fruit flies have these kinds of sensors on their antennae, while the bodies of butterfly larvae may be covered in sensory hairs which they use to hear, touch and taste. Some ears can pick up sounds a long way off, while others only operate over very short distances. It's sometimes difficult to say what 'hearing' actually is: for example, are you hearing or feeling when you pick up vibrations in the stem of the stalk of grass you're perched on?

If you are small, you can use an amplifier to boost your sound – like the insects commonly known as death-watch beetles (*Xestobium rufovillosum*). In the olden days, people thought that the sound they made was a fore-warning of imminent death, but the actual explanation is much more prosaic. These beetles live out their larval existence in rotting woodwork, often in the timbers of houses. As adults, the beetles find themselves partners simply by banging their heads against a wall. The sound transmits effectively through the woodwork and is picked up by both the beetles and us humans. This repetitive knocking is reminiscent of a ticking clock, or perhaps even more like somebody drumming their fingers impatiently on a table. According to ancient superstition these sounds meant somebody would die soon: they were a clock counting down a person's final hours, or the Grim Reaper waiting restlessly. Most probably, the fact is that it was just easier for people to hear these sounds at night in a quiet house, when, say, they were keeping watch at somebody's deathbed.

Fiddling on the World's Tiniest Violin

There are other insect sounds that we hear distinctly even in the clear light of day, like the song of the cicadas. Even so, cicadas aren't the winners in the competition for the world's noisiest insect. Adjusted for size, an aquatic insect a mere 2 millimetres long is the one most likely to walk away with the prize. Because the male of the water boatman species, part of the *Micronectidae* family, competes for the females' attention by making music. But how are you supposed to serenade your sweetheart when you're the size of a coarse-ground peppercorn? Well, the little water boatman does it by playing himself, using his abdomen as a string and his penis as a bow.

A couple of years ago, a team of scientists set up underwater microphones to record the song of French male water boatmen – the first-ever bootleg recording of this serenade. And what a hit it was, in its way! The scientists believed they could prove that these tiny creatures with their fiddling penises exceeded all bounds of reason when it came to sound production. An average sound level of no less than 79 decibels made by a critter a mere 2 millimetres in length: on land that's equivalent to the sound of a freight train passing by at a distance of around 50 feet.

It seems almost beyond the realms of possibility, and it may actually not be true either, because it's a complicated business comparing sounds underwater and in the air. Perhaps the water boatman will turn out not to be the world's noisiest insect after all. But the fact that it fiddles with its own penis – well, you can't take *that* away from it.

Tongues Beneath their Feet

Imagine if you could walk barefoot through the forest in summertime and actually *taste* the blueberries in the bushes as you stepped on them. This is what houseflies do – they taste with their feet. And flies are unbelievably hypersensitive, apparently a hundred times more sensitive to sugar than we are with our tongues.

But there are a few disadvantages to being a fly, on top of being a mostly unwanted creature to begin with. They don't have teeth or any other equipment that would enable them to eat solid food, which dooms them to an eternally liquid diet. So what is a poor housefly to do when it lands on something tasty, like your slice of bread? Well, it uses digestive enzymes from its belly to turn the food into a smoothie. To do so, the fly has to regurgitate some of its gastric juices onto the food, which isn't so great for us humans because it means that bacteria from the fly's last meal – possibly far from anything we'd classify as food – may end up on our slice of bread. But it's great for the fly, who can now suck up the food. The housefly's mouth is like a spongy vacuum cleaner head on a short shaft. The whole thing is attached to a kind of pump in the head, which creates suction, allowing the fly to hoover up the yummy nutritious soup.

Houseflies' poor table manners and somewhat varied diet, which includes items such as animal dung, are the reasons why they spread infection. The flies aren't dangerous in themselves, but like used syringes, they can carry infections and pass them on to us.

And now I think about it, maybe it's just as well we humans taste with our tongue and not our feet. Blueberry shrubs are one thing, but the thought of going around tasting the insides of your shoes all winter long is hardly appealing.

A Multifaceted Life

Insects' senses are adapted to their environment and needs. Whereas dragonflies and flies need good vision, cave-dwelling insects may be totally blind. Insects that come into close contact with flowers, like honeybees, can also see colours, but their colour spectrum is shifted upwards so that they don't see red light. On the other hand, they can see ultraviolet light, unlike us humans. This means that many flowers we see as monotone, such as sunflowers, have distinctive patterns for a bee, often in the form of 'landing strips' that direct them towards the source of nectar in the flower.

Insects' compound eyes consist of many individual eyes. The brain merges all the tiny pictures together into a single large image, although it is coarser and fuzzier than the way we humans see the world (it looks a bit like a low-res photograph on your PC screen when you've zoomed in too close). There are plenty of reasons why insects don't have driving licences, of course, but sight is a big one: they would never be able to read a road sign at 20 metres as the image would be too blurry. That said, their vision is supremely adapted to the tasks that will fill their days. Take whirligig beetles, for example: shiny black pearls of beetles that dash around on the surface of the waters of our lakes. They have two pairs of eyes, with different refraction: one pair for seeing clearly underwater so that they can watch out for hungry perch, and another for seeing clearly above the water so that they can find food on the surface.

Insects can also see a property to which we humans are blind: polarised light. This has to do with which plane the light is oscillating in, and it alters when sunlight is reflected – in the atmosphere or on a shining surface like water. But let's go easy on the physics and restrict ourselves to saying that insects use polarised light as a compass that enables them to orientate themselves. We humans only relate to polarised light when we put on a pair of Polaroid sunglasses to reduce the glare of reflected light.

In addition to having compound eyes, insects may also have separate simple eyes, whose main function is to distinguish between light and dark. Next time you encounter a stinging wasp, look deep into its eyes and note how, in addition to the compound eyes on either side of its head, it has three simple eyes in a neat triangle on its forehead.

The World's Most Skilful Hunter Sees You and You and You ...

When it comes to having eyesight adapted to their daily business, dragonflies are in a class of their own: their vision is a major reason why these insects are deemed to be among the world's most efficient predators.

Lions may put on an impressive display when hunting in a pride, but the fact is that they only manage to chase down their prey one in every four times. Even the great white shark, with its terrifying 300-toothed grin, fails in half of all its attempted attacks. The dragonfly, however, excels as a lethal hunter, succeeding in more than 95 per cent of its attempts.

Part of the reason why dragonflies are such skilled hunters is their extraordinary command of the skies. Their four wings can move independently of one another, which is unusual in the insect world. Each wing is powered by several sets of muscles, which adjust frequency and direction. This enables a dragonfly to fly both backwards and upside down, and to switch from hovering motionless in the air to speeding off at a maximum speed of close to 50 kilometres an hour. No wonder the US Army uses them as models when designing new drones. But their vision also makes a significant contribution to their success. And it is perhaps hardly surprising that they have good eyesight when almost their entire head consists of eyes. In reality, each eye is made up of 30,000 small eyes, which can see both ultraviolet and polarised light as well as colours. And since the eyes are like balls, the dragonfly can see most of what is happening on all sides of its body.

Its brain is also prepped for super-sight. When we humans see a rapid sequence of images, we see them in a

flowing movement, a film, if there are more than around 20 images per second. However, a dragonfly can see up to 300 separate images per second and interpret every single one of them. In other words, a cinema ticket would be quite wasted on a dragonfly. Where you and I see a moving film, it would simply see a very rapid slide show – one long stream of separate snapshots or frames.

The dragonfly brain is also capable of focusing over time on one specific section of the enormous quantity of visual impressions being received. They have a kind of selective attention that is unknown among other insects. Imagine you're travelling across the sea in a boat and see another boat ahead of you, at a given angle to you. If you ensure that you always have the boat at exactly the same angle in your field of vision, you will end up meeting. In a somewhat similar way, the dragonfly brain can lock its attention on approaching prey, coordinating its speed and direction to ensure a strike – and yet another successful hunt. Intricate, well-designed sensory organs alone are not enough: you also need a brain that can process all the information as it streams in, seeking out relevant patterns and connections, and sending the correct messages out again to different parts of the body. And even though insects have tiny little brains, we will see that they are a lot smarter than we might assume.

Go to the Ant and Be Wise

Carl Linnaeus, the great Swedish biologist who classified our species, placed insects in a separate group, in part because he believed they didn't have brains at all. Maybe that's not such a surprise, because if you behead a fruit fly, it can live pretty much as normal for several days, flying, walking and mating. Eventually, of course, it will starve to death, because no mouth means no food. The reason why insects can survive in a headless state is that they don't just have a main brain in their heads but also a nerve cord running through their entire body, with 'mini brains' in each joint. Consequently, many functions can be performed regardless of whether or not the head is in place.

Are insects intelligent? Well, that depends on what you mean by intelligence. According to Mensa, intelligence is the 'ability to acquire and analyse information'. Now, it's unlikely that anybody's going to argue that insects deserve to be members of Mensa, but the fact is that they never cease to surprise us with their ability to learn and make judgements. Some things we believed to be the sole preserve of large vertebrates with proper brains also turn out to be within the capabilities of our tiny friends.

But not all insects are created equal, and there are great differences between them. Those with dull lives and simple habits are the least bright. You don't need the wisdom of

Solomon if you're going to spend most of your life snugly tucked up in an animal hide with your sucking snout stuck in a vein. However, if you're a honeybee, a wasp or an ant, you're more in need of intelligence. The cleverest insects are the ones who look for food in lots of different places and also form close bonds with one another; in other words, the ones that live alongside many others in a community. These critters must constantly be making judgements: is that yellow thing over there a flower with sweet nectar or is it a peckish crab spider? Will I be able to carry that conifer needle alone or will it take several of us? Do I need to take a sip of this nectar to keep myself going, or should I take it home to Mum?

The social insects divide up jobs, share experiences and 'talk to each other' in an advanced way. This requires capacity for thought. To cite Charles Darwin in *The Descent of Man*: 'The brain of an ant is one of the most marvellous atoms of matter in the world, perhaps more so than the brain of a man.' And that was without knowing what we now know: that ants are capable of teaching skills to other ants.

The ability to *teach* has long been seen as exclusive to us humans, almost a proof of an advanced society. Three quite specific criteria distinguish teaching from other communications: it must be an activity that only happens when a teacher meets an 'ignorant' pupil; it must involve a cost for the teacher; and it must make the pupil learn more rapidly than he/she otherwise would have. The term is used for communication about concepts and strategies, so the honeybees' dance (*see page 28*), which is more about process, is generally not viewed as teaching. However, it turns out that ants are capable of teaching things to other ants, through a process known as 'tandem running', in which an experienced ant shows the way to food. This occurs in a European species, *Temnothorax albipennis*, which relies on landmarks such as trees, stones and others, as well as scent trails, to remember the way from the anthill to a new source of food. In order for several ants to be able to find the food, a she-ant (all worker ants are female, *see pages 52–3*) who knows the way must teach it to the others. The teacher runs on ahead to show the way, but constantly stops to wait for her pupil, who runs more slowly, apparently because she needs time to take note of the landmarks they are passing. When the pupil is ready again, she touches the teacher with her antennae and they continue on their journey. The behaviour therefore satisfies the three criteria of 'genuine teaching': the activity happens only when a teacher meets an 'ignorant' pupil, it involves a cost for the teacher (she must stop and wait) and it makes the pupil learn more quickly than she would have on her own.

Bumblebees have also recently been inducted into the exclusive little group of creatures who can teach tricks to their peers. Swedish and Australian scientists successfully trained bumblebees to pull on a string to gain access to nectar. They made artificial blue flowers in the form of plastic discs, which they filled with sugar water. When these were covered with a transparent plate of plexiglass, the only way of gaining access to the sugar water was to pull on a string attached to the fake flower. If the scientists only let untrained bumblebees loose on the covered flowers, they didn't understand a thing: none of them pulled on the string. A great starting point. Then the bumblebees were given a chance to get acquainted with the 'flowers', learning about the reward they offered. Gradually, the fake flowers were pushed further and further beneath the transparent plexiglass plate. This time, when the fake flowers were finally pushed fully beneath the plate, 23 out of 40 bumblebees began to pull on the string. In this way, they drew the fake flowers out and were able to suck up the sugar water. Admittedly it was a long lesson: the whole business took a good five hours of training per bumblebee.

The next step was to see whether these trained bumblebees could teach others their peculiar trick. Three bumblebees were selected as 'teachers'. New, untrained bumblebees were placed with them in a small transparent cage close to the flowers to watch and learn. Fifteen of the 25 'pupils' .grasped the point by watching how their teacher did it, and they too managed to pull out their reward when they got to have a go afterwards. All in all, this experiment showed both that the bumblebees could learn this rather unnatural skill and that they were capable of teaching the strategy to others.

Clever Horse Hans and the Even Cleverer Bee

Hans the Horse of Germany was a global celebrity in the early 1900s. He couldn't just count, he could also calculate – or so people thought. The horse could add, subtract, multiply and divide. He answered arithmetic problems by banging out the correct answer with his foreleg, and his owner, maths teacher Wilhelm von Osten, was convinced that the animal was just as clever as himself. In the end, it turned out that Hans couldn't calculate at all or even count. That said, he *was* a whiz at reading the minuscule signals in his questioner's body language and facial expressions. The person setting the problem had to count too, to make sure that Hans was giving the right answer, and a tiny, unconscious signal he made when the horse reached the correct number was all that Hans needed. In fact, not even the psychologist who eventually unmasked Hans was able to control these signals.

However, bees actually can count according to new research. Not very far, and they are no more capable of the four types of calculation than Hans was. Even so, it's a pretty impressive feat for a creature with a brain the size of a sesame seed. To measure this, honeybees were placed in a tunnel and trained to expect a reward after passing a certain number of landmarks, regardless of how far they had to fly. It turned out that bees could count up to four, and once they had learnt to do that, they were able to count the landmarks even if they were a new type they had never seen before.

And bees aren't just good at maths (well, considering their size), they are also good at languages.

Dancing Bee People

At around the same time as von Osten and his not-so-clever horse were alive, a future Nobel Prize winner was growing up in the neighbouring country of Austria. Even as a child Karl von Frisch loved animals and his mother must have been extremely tolerant, since she put up with the abundant array of wild creatures he brought home as pets. Over the course of his childhood, he noted 129 different pets in his journal, including 16 birds, 20-odd types of lizard, snakes and frogs, and 27 different fish. Later, as a zoologist, he was especially interested in fish and their colour vision. But almost by chance – largely because his aquatic research subjects displayed an unfortunate tendency to kick the bucket on the way to the conferences where he was supposed to be demonstrating his experiments – he switched to studying bees instead.

Karl von Frisch made two major discoveries: he proved that bees can see colours and that they can tell each other where to find food by performing a sophisticated dance. This was what won him a Nobel Prize in 1973. Von Frisch showed that when a honeybee finds a rich source of nectar, she returns home to the others and tells them where the flowers are. She dances in a kind of figure-of-eight, waggling her rear and vibrating her wings in the parts of the dance when she is moving in a straight line. The speed of the dance communicates the distance to the flowers, while the direction she dances in, in relation to a vertical line, describes where the flowers are relative to the position of the sun.

Today, bees' dance language is one of the most well-researched and best-mapped examples of animal communication, but history could have turned out quite differently. In Hitler's Germany, this research was nearly brought to a halt when it had barely begun. In the 1930s, when Karl von Frisch was working at the University of Munich, Hitler sympathisers scoured the university's employee roster to root out Jewish workers. When von Frisch's maternal grandmother proved to have been Jewish, he was fired from his post. But he was rescued by a tiny parasite – a parasite that caused a disease in bees that was in the process of wiping out Germany's bee population. Beekeepers and colleagues managed to persuade the Nazi leadership that von Frisch's future research was crucial if German beekeeping was to be rescued. The country was at war and in dire need of all and any foodstuffs farming could produce. A collapse of the honeybee population was unthinkable. Thus, von Frisch was able to carry on his research regardless, to the benefit of both bee knowledge and von Frisch's career.

I've Seen That Face Before

For a long time, we believed that only mammals and birds were capable of distinguishing between individuals, the very foundation of the capacity to develop personal relationships. This belief persisted until an enquiring scientist, with the help of some model aeroplane paints, began face-painting wasps. The species concerned was *Polistes fuscatus*, an American member of the family of paper wasps. Paper wasps build nests from chewed-up wood fibre, which look like a rosette of small larval cells. The nest hangs on a stalk, like an upside-down umbrella. Unlike regular stinging wasps, which also build nests from wood pulp, paper wasps' nests do not have a protective envelope around the comb of larval cells.

This wasp lives in a strictly hierarchical society, where it's crucial to know who's the boss. Maybe that's why they're so good with faces. A wasp whose face had been painted in a way that altered her pattern of stripes met with an aggressive reception from her fellow inhabitants when she returned to the nest. They didn't recognise her and were confused. As a control, the scientists also painted other wasps without altering their personal patterns. These wasps did not experience any reactions on their return to the nest.

Another fascinating point is that after a few hours of jostling, the other inhabitants of the nest got used to the face-painted wasp's new look. The aggression diminished and everything went back to normal. The other wasps had learned that this was indeed the same old Waspella, despite her makeover. This implies that the wasps actually have the capacity to recognise and distinguish between individual members of their community by their detailed facial cues or 'features'.

Honeybees take the whole business up a few notches: they can distinguish between human faces in the form of photographic portraits. What's more, they can remember a face they've become familiar with for at least two days. It is doubtful whether the bees relate to *what* they are actually seeing. They seem to believe the portraits they are presented with are really funny flowers, with the darker areas of eyes and mouth representing recognisable patterns on 'petals' that are actually the outline of the portrayed face.

This is new and exciting information, which forces us to rethink how facial recognition actually works: after all, we're saying that a creature whose brain is smaller than the letter 'o' in this book is able to achieve similar things to us humans, with our cauliflower-sized brainboxes. Greater understanding of these processes may be able to help people who suffer from face blindness (prosopagnosia), which is a neurological disorder characterised by the inability to recognise faces.

Perhaps this knowledge can also be used in surveillance – at airports, say. Not by installing a glass cage of buzzing bees to scrutinise us sternly as we go through customs (although that would be pretty cool!), rather by translating the principles that enable bees to recognise facial patterns into a logic that computers can follow. One hope is that this could lead to improved automatic facial recognition – of, say, wanted criminals – via surveillance cameras in crowded places.

What Shall We Call the Beetle?
Names and Insect Groups

In an attempt to organise the hordes of tiny critters, we humans have split them into groups according to how closely related they are. It's an ingenious system that starts with the *kingdom*, which is then divided into *phylum* and *class*, which are again divided into *order*, *family* and *genus* before we come to *species*.

Take the common wasp, for example. It is a species that belongs to the animal kingdom, the arthropod phylum, the insect class, the Hymenoptera order, the stinging wasp family, the *Vespula* genus and, finally, the common wasp species.

All species have a two-part Latin name, which is written in italics. The first part tells you which genus the species belongs to and the second additional part identifies the species. This system, introduced by Swedish naturalist Carl Linnaeus in the 1700s, makes it easier for biologists to be certain that they're talking about the same species even when communicating across national borders and language barriers. The common wasp has been given the name of *Vespula vulgaris*. You can often grasp the meaning of the Latin names: for example, *vulgaris* means 'common' (and is also the origin of the word *vulgar*).

Sometimes, the Latin name may tell us something about the insect's appearance, as with the *Stenurella nigra* beetle, where *nigra* describes the colour of this totally black species. Other times, the name may have been borrowed from mythology, as in the case of the beautiful peacock butterfly, *Aglais io*. Io was one of Zeus's mistresses, who also lent her name to one of Jupiter's moons.

With hundreds of thousands of insects to name, entomologists sometimes go a bit wild, calling species after their favourite artists, such as the *Scaptia beyonceae* horsefly (*see page 51*), or characters from much-loved films, like the *Polemistus chewbacca, P. vaderi,* and *P. yoda* wasps. Sometimes the species names contain a pun that you only discover when you say them out loud. Just try pronouncing the names of the bean-shaped beetle *Gelae baen* and *Gelae fish*, or the parasitic wasp *Heerz lukenatcha* and its relative *Heerz tooya*!

Orders for Order

There are around 30 different orders of insects in the world. Beetles, wasps, butterflies, flies and true bugs are the five largest. Other orders include dragonflies, cockroaches, termites, Orthoptera (grasshoppers and crickets), caddisflies, stoneflies, mayflies, thrips, lice and fleas.

Let's start with beetles (Coleoptera) – one of the largest orders of insects worldwide, despite tough competition from the wasp order, where improved knowledge is leading to a steady rise in the number of species. The hallmark of beetles is that their forewings are hard, forming a protective shell over their back. Beyond that, beetles are incredibly varied in appearance and lifestyle, and can be found on both land and water. There are more than 170 different beetle families, some of the largest being true weevils, scarab beetles, leaf beetles, ground beetles, rove beetles, longhorn beetles and jewel beetles. All in all, there are around 380,000 known beetle species worldwide.

The wasp order (Hymenoptera) consists of familiar insects such as ants, bees, bumblebees and stinging wasps, including many species that are social and live in colonies containing hordes of female workers and one or more queens. The order also encompasses many lesser-known sawflies and a huge number of parasitic wasp species. So far, we have identified more than 115,000 species in this order, but the number is rising steadily and this is probably the largest order of insects.

Butterflies and moths (of the Lepidoptera order) have wings covered in tiny scales arranged like roof tiles. There are more than 170,000 Lepidopteran species in the world, but many are small and unassuming. The best known are of course butterflies – comprising around 100 large, diurnal (as opposed to nocturnal) species that are often beautifully coloured and patterned. The nocturnal species are known as moths.

Flies, or Diptera, include not only species we commonly call flies, like blow flies and horseflies, but also mosquitoes, gnats and crane flies. Their Latin name derives from the fact that they have only two wings (*di* means two, *ptera* means wing), whereas insects normally have four, as mentioned earlier. In Dipterans, the hindwings have been repurposed as small, club-shaped gadgets that help them achieve balance in flight. We know of at least 150,000 species of Dipterans worldwide.

Most people are less familiar with the order of true bugs (Hemiptera), even though it encompasses more than 80,000 species. The group includes a variety of different-looking insects, like shield bugs, stinkbugs, bedbugs, pond skaters, cicadas, aphids and scale insects. They all have beak-shaped mouths that serve as a kind of drinking straw they use to suck up their food – often sap from plants, although a few are predators or blood-suckers. So, although we commonly use the word 'bug' to describe any sort of tiny critter, the true bugs are a specific group of insects.

And just so you know: spiders aren't insects. They belong to the same phylum, arthropods, but a separate class, arachnids, which they share with other creatures such as mites, scorpions and harvestmen (known as 'weaving women' in Norwegian because they move two of their eight legs as if they were pushing a shuttle to and fro across a loom).

Millipedes, centipedes and wood lice aren't insects either. To take the simplest hallmark, they all have too many legs and belong to various other groups of invertebrates. Nor are the super-cute springtails insects, despite having six legs, although they are *nearly* insects. That said, insect researchers are huge fans of a teeming, multi-legged community, so springtails and arachnids are often allowed into the fold when we discuss insects anyway. That is true in this book too.

CHAPTER 2

Six-legged Sex: Dating, Mating and Parenting

What accounts for the enormous success of insects as an animal group? Why are they so rich in species and why are there so very many of them? Put simply: because they are small, supple and sexy.

Life on our planet spans more than 10 orders of magnitude – from mycoplasma bacteria (measurable in nanometres) to the gigantic redwood trees of California, which can grow to heights of more than 100 metres. Insects can be found in six of these, all at the lower end of the scale – from wingless male fairy wasps, which are smaller than the cross section of a human hair, to stick insects the length of your forearm (*see page xxiii*). In other words, most insects are small, so they need only a tiny place to hide from their enemies and can exploit resources that are of no interest to larger creatures.

Insects are also unbelievably supple – in the sense that they are flexible and adaptable. Their wings allow them to disperse over areas that are extremely large in relation to their modest size, and their mastery of the three dimensions of airspace gives them access to a great many more sources of nutrition. The fact that most insects spend their childhood in a body shape totally different to their adult form (*see page 4*) means that they can exploit entirely different habitats and sources of food in the different stages of their lives – and the young do not compete with the adults for food.

Last but not least, insects have an astonishing capacity for reproduction. There must surely have been a fly on the wall who thought God was talking to her when He said 'Be fruitful, and multiply, and replenish the earth and subdue it!' (Genesis 1:28, New King James Version). Just listen to this: take two fruit flies and leave them in ideal living conditions for a year – equivalent to 25 generations for fruit flies. Every fruit fly mother lays 100 eggs. Let's say that they all grow to adulthood, and that half of them are females who mate and lay another 100 eggs. Once the year is over, you will be left with the 25th generation and that alone will amount to almost a septillion sweet little red-eyed fruit flies. A septillion is the figure 1 followed by 42 zeros. To make this figure more meaningful, imagine packing these flies together densely, as densely as possible, into one enormous fruit fly ball. You'd end up with a sphere whose diameter exceeded the distance between the Earth and the sun! It's a good thing these insects have so many enemies because otherwise there wouldn't be any room left on Earth for us humans.

Fortunately (we might say) most of the insect eggs will never catch so much as a glimpse of adult life. Most insects starve to death, are eaten or die in some other way long before they start a family. It's a harsh struggle. Over time, an incredible range of adaptations has come about, especially when it comes to choice of partner and propagation. We will look at some of them in this chapter.

50 Shades of Strange

Insects' senses are crucial to their quest to find a partner, and the competition here is tough. But the struggle is far from over when boy meets girl. On the contrary, it has barely begun, because the question of how to pass on as much of their genetic material as possible may have different answers for the two sexes. For example, it's not unusual for the female to mate with several males over a short period, and the male takes a dim view of this because it means that his sperm face competition. Consequently, many insects come equipped with a male sex organ reminiscent of a Swiss Army knife, complete with all sorts of imaginatively shaped scrapers, ladles and spoons. The purpose? To eliminate any sperm that got there before their own.

This toolkit also comes in handy if the previous male has resorted to another trick: plugging up the female's genital opening. The idea is to create a kind of homemade chastity belt that prevents the female from being able to mate again. The gambit is only partially effective, as male number two simply uses his scrapers, pike poles and hooks to remove the bung and gain access for his own equipment. So much for candlelight and tender caresses!

Another trick the male deploys is to ensure that as much of his sperm as possible is delivered to the female, and that she has as little time as possible available for other males. He does this by making their mating process as lengthy as possible. Some species take this to extremes: the Southern green shieldbug, *Nezara viridula*, which has spread all over the world, including to the UK as a stowaway on imported foodstuffs, can keep at it for 10 whole days. And that's still nothing compared with Indian stick insects, which have apparently been known to stay stuck together for an insane 79 days in an extreme sport version of tantric sex!

As well as engaging in prolonged mating, the male often keeps an eye on the female post-consummation. Have you ever seen those small blue damselflies, a close relative of the dragonfly, perching or flying around in

pairs? Sometimes the coupling creatures resemble a heart – although that doesn't imply any human notions of romance. The sole purpose of this tandem position is that it allows the male to keep watch on the female and make sure she doesn't mate with any rivals until she has laid (what he hopes are) their jointly fertilised eggs on a suitable aquatic plant.

These highly demanding competitive conditions make it vital to keep your equipment in order. And the tiny fruit fly *Drosophila bifurca* is one insect whose equipment is beyond reproach. This little critter, a close relative of the same fruit flies that drive you crazy in your kitchen, is the proud holder of the record for the world's longest sperm: at almost 6 centimetres long, it is 20 times longer than the creature itself. For men, that would be equivalent to having sperm the length of a handball court! How is it even possible?

The answer is that the whole thing consists largely of a thin tail bundled up into a ball. Enlarged photographs of the sperm look a bit like what happens when the kids make dinner and forget to put enough water in the spaghetti pan. So, what's the point? Well, the long sperm are the fruit fly reproductive system's answer to Usain Bolt: the longest sperm outcompete the shorter and are more likely to win the race to fertilise an egg.

And since we're in the realm of the bizarre, there's no

getting away from bedbugs – those blood-sucking rascals that hide out in cracks in the wall and beds in flats and hotels the whole world over. When darkness falls, out they shuffle to poke their sucking snouts into you as you sleep. They're definitely not the kind of souvenir you want to bring back from your holidays, but the fact is that bedbugs are a growing problem, all over the world. In part this is because we travel a lot, but the main reason is that bedbugs have developed resistance to the most common insecticides, so that they no longer kill them.

At any rate, the point in this context is that the males of certain true bug species, including bedbugs, skip anything resembling foreplay; they can't even be bothered to find the female's genital opening but simply stick their sex organ into her belly and leave the sperm to find their way through the orifice to the egg cells. This often injures the female, preventing her from being able to mate with any other partners. In this way, the male attempts to ensure that he will be the father of her child. That said, the female has evolved a reinforced area on her belly where the male most often punctures her, which limits her injuries. This illustrates an important point: the battle of the sexes involves two warring parties and both sexes fight for what is most advantageous to them from an evolutionary point of view.

Ladies' Choice

It's possible that early insect researchers, almost exclusively men, tended to see everything from the male perspective. Be that as it may, the fact is that modern research yields ever more examples of how female insects also work to advance their own interests.

One such example is the way certain females simply gobble up the male once they've finished mating. This is most common among spiders, distant relatives of insects. The male American fish spider, for example, dies in the middle of the act. This is because his sex organ bursts once he's delivered his sperm (or to put it in dry scientific terms: 'We observed that mating results in obligate male death and genital mutilation'). And then he gets eaten – for the sake of the children. Even though his chosen one is a chubster 14 times his weight, his little body still provides a useful protein boost. A little extra food comes in handy when you're preparing to lay hundreds of spider eggs.

The praying mantis is also famed for what is known as sexual cannibalism. That said, field studies have demonstrated that the male ends up on the supper menu more rarely when he mates in natural surroundings than in artificial, laboratory conditions. However, the insect mum has plenty of other tricks up her sleeve: it turns out that she can secretly control which males get to father her children.

A great many mechanisms come into play here; the sperm's quest to reach the egg is more like an obstacle race than a gentle dip in calm waters. Since it is common for the sperm to be stored in a special 'sperm bank' inside the female, for the actual fertilisation of her eggs to happen at a later stage she has several ways of influencing which sperm to save and use.

One scientist carried out a cunning if brutal experiment to demonstrate this. She split a pile of flour beetles into two groups. Half the males were put on a starvation diet to make them look like weak specimens with poor genetic quality. Of the females, the scientist simply killed half so that they couldn't influence the outcome. When the scientist put the beetles together, both the starved and the well-fed males mated away with living and newly defunct females, of which there were equal numbers. And now the really clever bit: the scientist found that the internal sperm banks of the dead females contained just as much sperm from the hungry, poor-quality males as from the well-fed, high-quality males. Those of the living females, however, contained a great deal more sperm from the high-quality males. This indicates that the female was taking active measures to control the whole process and ensure that the strong, high-quality males would father her children.

Life Without Men?

There are plenty of ways to solve the conundrum of ensuring that 'generation shall follow generation', and insects
offer several examples of most options. Sexual reproduction, which requires both a male and a female, is the most
common – among insects too. But many insects can opt for
the single life and still continue their line. In fact, several
insects are periodic practitioners of virgin birth. Female
aphids, for example, can use this method to achieve a
quick, effective baby boom on your rosebush in the spring.
They don't have time to hang around and wait for their
eggs to hatch, so they simply give birth to living aphid
babies, from egg cells that develop into new individuals
without being fertilised. And that's not all: in some aphid
species, the females can be like Russian dolls – they contain baby aphids that are themselves already carrying new
female aphids!

No wonder your rosebush is teeming with life! Despite
the absence of men, it's questionable whether we can accu-
rately call this 'the single life'. Soon there won't be enough
room for all of them on the same bush. Up until now, the
ladies have been wingless but now it's time to squeeze out
a few winged females who can fly over to the neighbouring
bush and continue the mass production there.

When the days grow shorter, the temperatures fall and

autumn is on the way, another change is triggered. The aphid ladies switch to production of males *and* females. These then mate and this time the female lays eggs – the only way that aphids can survive the winter. She places her eggs on a suitable perennial plant. When spring comes, the eggs will hatch new virgin-birthing females. And the game is on again.

So why is there actually any need for men if, in a single season, an aphid lady can be sole progenitor of more children, grandchildren, great-grandchildren and so on than there are humans on the planet? Wouldn't it be more productive if all individuals were able to produce offspring rather than just half of them? (Not to mention all the time saved if there were no need to worry about dating ...)

Biologists have long been interested in the question of why most animals and plants come in two sexes, and the discussion is still ongoing. One disadvantage with virgin births is that all the individuals are genetically identical, which leaves species less room for manoeuvre if environmental conditions happen to change. Consequently, sexual reproduction, which blends the genetic material of two individuals, is a good and necessary means of promoting genetic variation and weeding out harmful mutations. Another handy thing about having two sexes is that it also allows species to rely on different strategies: one sex may have few but large and nutritious sex cells – egg cells

– while the other may have many small mobile sex cells – sperm cells.

Long Live the Queen!

Aphids aren't the only insects who live in a thoroughly female-dominated society. It is extremely likely that every single ant, stinging wasp and honeybee you've ever seen was female. With very few exceptions, at any rate.

Do you remember *Bee Movie*, the film about Barry, the male bee who gets bored of life as a factory worker in the beehive? Biologically speaking, it's all wrong. So, for that matter, is Shakespeare's *Henry V*, in which he describes how the many inhabitants of the beehive are overseen by a bee king. The worker bees in the beehive aren't males, nor are they ruled by a king bee.

The ladies are the ones who decide and do all the important work in the world of the honeybees. All the worker bees are female and their ruler is a queen. The males, the drones, only live for a short period in the autumn and have just one role: to mate with a new queen. The male bees don't even gather their own food but are fed by the female workers.

Now perhaps we can forgive Shakespeare, DreamWorks, and the other people who have got this so badly wrong, as the misconception is old and hard to put to rest. The

Ancient Greeks tried to find out about the lives of bees but just couldn't get it all to add up. After all, they knew that normal honeybees had stings – and surely women couldn't come equipped with such a formidable weapon? And if the short-tempered stingers were women then the large, sluggish individuals who couldn't even be bothered to collect nectar must be men, and that just couldn't be the case, could it?

It wasn't until the end of the 1600s, when microscopes came into use in dissection, that it became possible to establish that, yes, the tireless, terrifying workers and their monarch were all women, and the idlers were men. But it would be another 200 years before people truly understood how bees came into the world, because nobody had ever seen a honeybee having sex. The prevailing theory in those days was that the male bees, the dozy drones, engaged in the whole process at a respectful distance, remotely fertilising their queen with what was fancifully referred to as 'sperm odour'.

Only in the late 1700s was it discovered that queen bees who had been out for a flutter returned to the hive with a male sex organ attached to their own genital opening. These are the remnants of the lucky winner, selected from a swarm of drones who have chased her. The queen often mates with several members of the swarm. She saves up all the sperm cells (as many as 100 million) in a special internal sperm bank and doles them out as needed over the rest of her life.

For the drone, however, mating is the last thing he will do with his life. The actual transmission of sperm is nothing short of an explosion – so powerful that the drone's sex organ splits open and is torn loose from his abdomen, and he dies shortly afterwards. A bit like a miniature version of 'comes in like a lion, goes out like a lamb'. It's so extreme that it has even inspired the tabloids to devote a few column inches to insects, accompanied by headlines like this one from *The Sun*: 'Male bees' testicles EXPLODE when they reach orgasm'.

Beyoncé Was Right

From the bees' queen to the woman today's music fans call Queen B – American pop diva Beyoncé Knowles. Insects got a PR boost from an unexpected quarter a few years ago when media platforms worldwide broke the news that a new species of horsefly had been discovered and named after Beyoncé: *Scaptia beyonceae*.

There are two reasons why the Beyoncé horsefly got its name: first, because it was originally collected in 1981, the year of her birth, although it wasn't confirmed or named until long afterwards; secondly, and more importantly, because it had such a beautiful backside. The trimming of golden hairs on its rump reminded the scientists tasked with naming the species of the artist's own rear end when encased in tight, glittering diva dresses. (I eagerly await the day when there are more of us women entomologists, so we can start naming insects for their broad, manly winged shoulders or their ripped abs ...)

I'm not sure how flattered Beyoncé was, if indeed she was even aware of the whole business, considering that the horsefly concerned was from inland Australia. Although horseflies are flower visitors and contribute to pollination, they are primarily known as nuisances to people and domestic animals; it hurts when they take a chunk out of us, they stress animals out and they can transmit disease. At any rate, around the same time as all this was going on, Beyoncé had a major hit that asked the question: 'Who run the world?' Perhaps you know the answer: girls!

I don't think for a second that Beyoncé had insects in mind when she sang this. But she might just as well have done. Because if we count up all the male and female animals on the planet, insects are responsible for ensuring that there are more girls on Earth. If we ignore bacteria, hermaphrodites and other organisms without any clear gender and study the proportion of females among the remaining animals, some extremely abundant groups, such as insects, are notably dominated by females. The honeybee workers are women, all 83 billion of them. All ant workers are women, and there are enormous numbers of ants on planet Earth; although there is no agreement over an exact figure, the BBC believes it is safe to assume that ants are the most abundant type of insect on the planet. And other fairly abundant insect species, such as aphids, may be female dominated at certain times of the year (*see page 47*).

Could this female domination on land be offset by aquatic species? The sea contains small crustaceans, the aquatic counterparts of insects, which dominate in number terms – creatures like *Calanus finmarchicus* and other types of copepods. The sex distribution among these is more equal, but in this group, too, scientists sometimes report an excess of females. Even among farmed cattle and poultry, which have a large presence on the planet, bulls and roosters are normally outnumbered by their female counterparts. Okay, there are also some organisms that typically have an excess of males, including some flatworms and tortoises, but it is unlikely that this is enough to help correct the imbalance. So, it looks as if Queen B was right in a way. Calculated by the number of total individuals, 'girls' really are the ones who make the world go round, thanks to insects and the extreme dominance of females in the most successful species.

I Am Fatherless but Still Have a Grandfather

How can social insects such as honeybees, ants and many wasp species form societies with such skewed sex distribution? Part of the secret lies in how the sex of the offspring is determined in these insects. For human beings and many other insects, sex chromosomes determine the whole business, but these kinds of insects don't have sex chromosomes.

Sex is determined by whether the egg is fertilised or not – and the queen is the one to decide that. She's the only one allowed to lay eggs. If she fertilises the egg with the sperm she has saved up from the swarming, it becomes a female – a worker or a queen, depending on the nourishment it receives during the larval stage. If she lays an unfertilised egg, it becomes a male.

This system leads to some genetic peculiarities, especially if the queen has only mated with one male in her life. Because in that case, the queen's daughters will be more closely related to their sisters than to any offspring they themselves might have! Put simply, this is because every one of the bee dad's sperms contains exactly the same genetic material, so all his daughters (he cannot have sons – remember, they only develop from unfertilised eggs) inherit identical genes from him. This makes it more advantageous for these daughters to opt out of having children themselves and instead help feed up more sisters, including new queens, simply because that strategy will enable them to pass on more of their own genetic material.

For a long time, people thought this provided a good explanation for the social insects' strange societies dominated by sterile workers, but we now know that honeybee queens usually mate with several males. And in termites, which are also social, sex is not determined by whether or not the egg is fertilised – so that explanation simply doesn't hold up. Impassioned debate continues over what other mechanisms might explain the phenomenon. At any rate, this strange system means that some unexpected challenges would arise if a male bee tried to draw his family tree. After all, he has no father, since he was born from an unfertilised egg. Yet he does have a grandfather, a maternal grandfather to be precise. Our human hobby of genealogy – involving my children, your children and our children – is a piece of cake by comparison!

Parental Leave the Insect Way

Insect mums generally consider their job to be done and dusted once the egg has been laid. But there are exceptions. Some insects are genuinely nurturing, providing variants of both bottle feeds and nappy changes. And these discoveries are incredibly useful beyond providing material for your next dinner party anecdote. By studying strategies used by related species that do and don't engage in childcare, or by manipulating species and observing the impact on the offspring's survival, biologists have learnt a great deal about ecology and evolution.

For example, there is a cockroach (*Diploptera punctata*) that gives birth to living young. This means that the eggs hatch inside her, so the nymphs must be fed some nutrients in order to grow up big and strong. Cockroaches don't have a warm, cosy uterus where their young are fed intravenously through an umbilical cord. Instead, the mother has special glands in her abdomen that excrete milk protein in liquid form. The nutritional content of this 'milk' is supposedly like battle rations – an optimal blend of proteins, carbohydrates and fat. Some claim it could become the new superfood for us humans too, but since it's pretty time-consuming milking cockroaches, we'll probably have to opt for producing the milk synthetically.

Another of our less popular insects, the deer fly, has a similar life cycle. A parasite that sucks deer blood, it swarms at the height of the mushroom-picking season. Although it rarely stings humans, it is annoying when masses of them land on you, shed their wings and crawl around in your hair. But for elks, they are a genuine problem. One elk that was examined by Norway's Veterinary Institute in 2007 was found to be infested with 10,000 deer flies.

Deer-fly eggs also hatch inside the mother and the fly larva is 'breastfed' through special glands inside the maternal body, while the mother sits snugly ensconced in the elk's fur. Her offspring are 'born' in the form of a sort of pupal cocoon, which becomes hard and black as an ebony bead, then falls off the elk and onto the ground. There it lies until it hatches the following autumn, when the cycle starts again.

Other insects also nurse and nurture their young. We have already taken a look at the social insects, where all the many sisters are employed as nannies for their younger siblings. And their mum is far from lazy, either. A termite queen drops a new egg every third second throughout her entire life so it's no wonder she needs help from their older siblings

Earwigs, those elongated brown insects with a pincer at the rear, are particularly affectionate mothers. While they may not exactly change nappies, they do keep watch over their eggs, cleaning away fungus spores and washing them with a substance that is assumed to inhibit the growth of mould and fungus. When the young first hatch, she fetches food and feeds the small nymphs. An experiment showed that earwig mums' tender care multiplied the eggs that hatched from 4 to 77 per cent. Sexton beetles are another example of caring parents (*see page 151*).

And it's not all about the mothers. In Scandinavia, we

are proud of our progress on the gender equality front. But when it comes to the smallest among us, other countries are streets ahead on this issue – maybe because there isn't a single representative of giant water bugs (Belostomatids) in Norway. Also known as toe-biters and electric light bugs, this subfamily contains a rare example of fathers being the ones who take parental leave. In fact, they take on a whole brood, from different mothers. After mating, the female lays her eggs in neat rows on the father's back, and it's his job to look after them, floating on the surface of the water and making sure that the eggs neither dry out nor drown. And the mother? Like Ibsen's Nora, she goes her own way.

Some insects will go to extreme and savage lengths to raise their young. Not by sticking around to look after them, but rather by making sure there is fresh meat waiting when the larva hatches – by placing the egg inside another living being. In the next chapter, we will look at some of the strange ways insects eat – and are eaten.

CHAPTER 3

Eat or Be Eaten:
Insects in the Food Chain

The recipe for a successful insect life is simple: you just have to stay alive long enough to reproduce. And to stay alive, you need food. Much of an insect's life consists of eating and not being eaten.

Many insects eat each other. If there are 50 ways to leave your lover, I can assure you that there are an awful lot more ways to eat other creatures – *including* your lover! You can eat them up from the inside or the outside; as eggs, larvae or adults. You can eat them using mandibles, sponges or drinking straws, or you can simply stop eating: quite a few insects only eat as larvae but don't feed at all as adults.

Since the done thing is to keep on the right side of life's brutal but simple eat-or-be-eaten rule, insects go to extremes to avoid being gobbled up by other creatures. They may live in hiding, concealing themselves through camouflage or by pretending to be something else – preferably something dangerous or inedible. They can opt to survive by disappearing in the crowd or by collaborating with others in ingenious ways. Insects' strategies for laying their hands on nutrition without becoming food themselves are an object lesson in jaw-dropping but often brutal adaptations, which it would be criminal of me to keep from you.

Darwin's Qualms

Take parasites, for example. Many insects are what we call parasitoids – parasites that ultimately kill their host. The host is often devoured from the inside out: the parasitoid larvae hatch inside an animal – for example, another insect – and slowly but surely eat their way through all its internal organs. The whole thing is elegantly done: the larvae leave the vital organs until last. Well, fresh meat is preferable, after all! The host usually dies once the parasitoid larvae have eaten their fill and are ready for adult life.

The natural historians and theologians of the 1800s tore their hair out when they found out about this – it just didn't fit in with their notion of a creation formed by a good and loving God. Darwin also struggled with it, writing to his American colleague Asa Gray in 1860: 'I cannot persuade myself that a beneficent and omnipotent God would have designedly created the Ichneumonidae with the express intention of their feeding within the living bodies of caterpillars.'

If only he had known! There are *much* worse things than that.

Zombies and Soul-suckers

The beautiful, green-eyed *Dinocampus coccinellae* is a parasite wasp. The female sticks her egg-laying tube (ovipositor) into a ladybird beetle and lays an egg. The egg hatches and over the next 20 days the wasp larva chews its way through many of the ladybird's inner organs. Then the larva nonchalantly squeezes its way out of the ladybird's abdomen somehow or other while the unfortunate host is still alive. The wasp larva spins itself a little ball of silk between the ladybird's legs, where it transforms into a pupa.

Something quite remarkable happens next: the ladybird's behaviour abruptly alters: it stops moving and just stands there, stock-still, like a living shield. But every time a hungry foe of wasps approaches, the ladybird gives a jerk, thereby scaring off anything that might consider eating the now-helpless monster that has just eaten her up. This lasts for a week until the wasp hatches and flies off, leaving the ladybird to her own devices.

The big question here is how the wasp mother can control the ladybird, transforming her into a zombie babysitter.

After all, several weeks have passed since she laid her egg and vanished. The answer is that the wasp mother doesn't just inject the ladybird with the egg but also with a virus. The virus accumulates in the brain and is controlled by a timing mechanism that paralyses the ladybird at the precise moment when the larva is squeezing its way out, so the virus enables the wasp to take over the brain of the ladybird, making it serve not just as baby food but also as a babysitter. The only good thing we can say about all this is that, unbelievably enough, the ladybird sometimes survives the whole ordeal.

The cockroaches that fall prey to the soul-sucker wasp aren't so lucky. You probably remember the dementors in *Harry Potter*, those flapping black monsters that suck out people's souls? That's what gave the *Ampulex dementor* wasp its name. It is one of several species in the cockroach wasp genus, a representative of which can even be found in Norway. During childhood, these wasps live inside cockroaches.

Here, too, the whole process starts with a mother who is out and about wielding her egg-laying stinger. First, she stings the cockroach in the chest to paralyse its legs for a few minutes – because the next stage involves high-level brain surgery, which requires 'the patient' to lie completely still. Now the wasp stings the head. With extreme precision, she places a dose of nerve poison in two specific points of the cockroach's brain. This blocks the signals that control its ability to start moving: the cockroach can still move but cannot itself take the initiative to set in motion. Now the cockroach is at the mercy of the wasp's will. And the wasp's will is to take the cockroach to a place where she can lay eggs on it. But since the cockroach is far too big for the wasp to carry, it's handy that it has now lost whatever cockroach free will it might once have possessed but is still able to walk. This allows the soul-sucking wasp to simply bite into the cockroach antennae and lead her prey wherever she wants – like a dog on a leash – straight to its death.

The cockroach is a biddable prey that allows itself to be led down into a hole in the ground; here, the wasp lays an egg, which it glues to the cockroach's leg. Then the soul-sucker wasp blocks the entrance to the hole with small stones and vanishes. Her little larva child spends the next month fattening itself up. First, it sucks the bodily fluids out of the cockroach's leg and then it bores into the creature's insides and gobbles up its intestines, before forming a pupa inside the cockroach, which eventually dies.

Ugh! Maybe Darwin was better off not knowing about this. It's difficult to see any goodness in such ruthless behaviour. Then again, evolution has never been driven by love and compassion.

Bold Hitchhikers

Some insects live off the young of other insects. The bold blister beetle eats bee larvae, yet is still able to hitch a ride with the parents, all the way into the nursery.

One May day as I was sitting out in the sunshine, a strange fat beetle came pottering across my garden table, shimmering and bluish-black. It looked as if it had borrowed a tailcoat three sizes too small for it: its abdomen was so full of eggs that it bulged out beyond the hind edge of the wings. It was a blister beetle paying a morning visit. In Norwegian, it's also known as spring beetle, May beetle or Easter beetle, and is as rich in adaptations as it is in names.

The plump lady beetle is the source of what must be the spring's strangest stowaway. In a little while, she'll dig a hole in the earth and squeeze out a load of eggs, maybe as many as 40,000. The eggs hatch into stressed little larvae with hefty hooks on all six legs. They look a bit like long narrow head lice, or wingless stoneflies, but filled with feverish energy. The triungulin larvae, as they are known, eventually gather in flowers and there they wait for life's great lottery draw.

The thing is, it is crucial for these larvae to end up in the right place if they are to have a shot at life. And they need a ride to get there. They hook onto the first insect that lands in their flower – but it's game over for all the larvae that hitch a ride with the wrong kind of bee. And this is precisely why so many eggs are needed in the first place: the only ones whose future is assured are the fortunate few who strike lucky and stow away on a wild bee heading in the right direction.

Blister beetle triungulins gather in a flower in such a way that they form a shape that resembles a bee. The larvae also emit scent signals that imitate the smell of a lonely female bee. A male bee soon comes a-wooing. As he tries to mate with what he thinks is a female bee, she disintegrates and the triungulin larvae climb up onto the male bee. When the bewildered male then flies on and, with luck, meets a real bee lady, the larvae hop onto *her* like rats leaving a sinking ship. That way, they are assured a lift home to her nest.

The triungulins repay their driver by shapeshifting into tiny legless larvae. They lie still in the nest, slurping up all their driver's pollen. And for dessert, they generally gobble up the wild bee larvae that are the rightful inhabitants of the nest. Once the blister beetle larvae are good and full, they pupate and wait for spring. That way, the cycle can start all over again.

Blister beetles owe their name to the fact that they secrete a blistering agent called cantharidin – one of the more poisonous substances known to man. An amount the weight of a grain of rice is enough to kill a human being.

For some reason or another, somebody got the (mistaken) idea that cantharidin was an aphrodisiac. Dried blister beetles of the 'Spanish fly' species (*Lytta vesicatoria*), which are found further south in Europe as well as in the east, were once used as a sexual stimulant for men. It is said that Livia, the scheming wife of Emperor Augustus (of Nativity story fame), sprinkled her male guests' food with crushed Spanish fly in the hope that this would make them cast aside all discretion and self-control, and do things she could later use against them.

In reality, the substance causes blisters and festering sores if it comes into contact with your skin, as well as painful irritations and swelling of the urethra if you eat it. What's more, there's an incredibly thin line between non-lethal and lethal effect – you don't want to mess with this stuff.

Blister beetles are adapted to emerge at the same time as the first flight of the solitary wild bees they parasitise. That's why you only see them in early spring. You're best off leaving a blister beetle to live out its peculiar life in peace if you happen to be lucky enough to spy one.

Insects That Sing for Their Supper

I'm not much good at cooking Sunday dinners. We've often been on a hike, and nobody feels much like cooking when we eventually get home. And we don't know what to make, either: we were in no state to think two whole days ahead when we did the shopping on Friday afternoon, exhausted after a hectic week.

Oh, to be an insect at a time like this! Or more precisely, a spotted predatory katydid, a big, bright-green Australian bush cricket. It would sort things out in a jiffy *and* make sure the food was delivered to the door, good and fresh. So fresh, in fact, that it would deliver itself.

All these katydids need to do is sing for their supper and it comes running, straight into the jaws of a poor soul starving for its Sunday dinner. What do they sing? Well, put it this way – it's along the lines of Romeo's serenade beneath the balcony. The katydid has learnt to imitate the mating signal of a totally different species, a classy cicada cutie, and this brings unsuspecting male cicadas strolling over. They head towards the sound but instead of finding a sweet fellow cicada, they encounter a hungry and much larger enemy: Sunday dinner has just served itself! In scientific language, this is called 'aggressive mimicry' – a process whereby a predator or a parasite imitates the signal of another species in order to exploit the recipient of the signal. There are several examples: the *Photuris versicolor* firefly, for instance, can imitate a total of 11 relatives and pass itself off as a hot-to-trot female of all these species. Thus, it is able to sit around idly, flashing away like a short-circuiting Christmas tree, and make its food come to it.

Even stranger is the bolas spider's home delivery system. These spiders spin a thread with a sticky lump at one end, which they swing round and round until it hits a passing moth. The moth is then hauled in like a fish on a hook and packed up neatly in silk to be digested in peace and quiet when the night is over. This hunting weapon is reminiscent of a bolas, the implement consisting of two heavy balls linked by a cord that is used by gauchos, Argentina's answer to the North American cowboy.

But it's one thing to be a gaucho on horseback throwing your bolas at an animal you're chasing down, quite another to be a spider, sitting stock-still. What are the actual chances of an owlet moth passing by the spot where you are sitting still, seemingly innocent, swinging your bolas? Roughly equal to zero. That's why this spider has also found a way to sing for its supper: it sings with scent. The bolas spider has learnt to imitate the complex scent signals of various species of moths. Sensing love is in the air, Mr Moth flies closer and closer to the source of this natural version of a femme fatale's scent ... until he finds himself stuck fast in the spider's trapping gear.

Robber Flies Deserve Their Own Day

There is a day for everything: we have the World Migratory Bird Day, the World Day of Happiness, we even have Waffle

Day and International Tea Day. But perhaps you didn't know that the last day of April every year is World Robber Fly Day. The creator of the #worldrobberflyday hashtag, Erica McAlister, is an insect specialist at the Natural History Museum in London. She thinks that we ought to celebrate insects a lot more than we do. And why not start with robber flies?

Robber flies (Asilidae family) are pretty hefty predators. The family includes species that are up to 6 centimetres in length, which is nothing short of gigantic by fly standards. Sun-loving, dark, often slender flies, with powerful legs, enormous eyes and a bushy moustache on their upper lip, they have full command of the air and can switch direction quickly or hover around waiting for unsuspecting prey to fly peacefully by. In the blink of an eye the prey is trapped by six powerful, hairy robber fly legs. Without bothering to land, the robber fly thrusts a solid proboscis into its prey, which may well be an insect larger than itself – in warmer parts, it may even be a humming bird. The robber fly injects its victim with a cocktail of spit, poison and digestive fluids, instantly transforming the innards of the trapped creature into a kind of insect smoothie served up in a handy beaker. A couple of swift slurps – generally at top speed – and the robber fly casts aside the empty shell. Not for nothing are these roughnecks also known as 'assassin flies'.

Many robber fly species are rare and we know little

about how they spend their larval phase. However, we do know that they are important in controlling other insect populations and keeping them down, so it might be wise to learn more about these hefty flying predators and their role in the food web.

Swarmageddon

Imagine a red-eyed army of insects crawling up out of the earth, slow and silent. Every insect is the size of your thumb and they emerge in such vast quantities that they call to mind a bad horror film about the end of the world. We're talking about a density of around three million insects on an area the size of a football pitch! But this is neither science fiction nor a doomsday prophecy, it is simply Swarmageddon – as some wits have dubbed the cyclical emergence of North America's 17-year cicadas.

These sap-sucking insects are quite content to forego the outdoor life for as many as 16 years in a row. Instead, they hide deep down in the dark alleyways and alcoves beneath the earth, where they lie silently waiting. Now and then they'll take a sip of a root-sap cocktail through the built-in drinking straw that serves as their mouth. Then, in year 17, the troops gather, preparing for some serious gatecrashing.

They emerge from the earth in their hordes: pale brown,

quiet and wingless. The silent assembly climbs up into the trees and embarks on its final moulting, which transforms the cicadas into adult individuals equipped for procreation. Voilà! Out of the old exoskeleton steps a winged being, all dressed up and ready to party. The pick-up sessions get under way, love is in the air, and silence is a thing of the past. If you've spent 17 years lying quietly in the earth, you've got plenty to say for yourself. We humans hear the cicadas' song as an intense, high-frequency, grating racket. Multiply that by millions of these singing male cicadas and it's no wonder people can suffer hearing loss if they spend too much time out and about when the 17-year cicadas strike. The sound level can be as high as 100 decibels. Although the 17-year cicada doesn't sting or bite, Americans have to cancel garden parties and open-air wedding ceremonies when Swarmageddon strikes, because it simply isn't possible for people to talk together outdoors while this is going on.

Still, the party is short-lived. After spending 99 per cent of their lives underground for 17 years, the cicadas' adult life is over in three to four weeks. Their song leads to mating and mating creates new cicada eggs. The eggs hatch over the course of a few weeks and small cicada nymphs crawl and crawl along the branch they were born on until it runs out and … boom! The newly hatched, wingless nymphs fall to earth and dig their way down – down into 17 years of darkness.

Long before the nymphs hatch, their mum and dad are dead, having fulfilled their role. Now the only thing left to do is for the Americans to fetch their snow shovels and clear kilograms of lifeless insect carcasses off their drives and verandas, and await the next appearance in 17 years' time – with anticipation or dread.

The 17-year cicadas are, in fact, the longest-lived insects we know of, along with their cousins, the 13-year cicadas. There are several species, each of which may have several broods with different 'timing' in different parts of the US. No wonder the Latin genus name of these peculiar insects is *Magicicada*.

Counting to 17

So what is the point of the 17-year cicada's astonishing life story? And how in the world do these insects manage to count?

It appears that this behaviour evolved because it reduces the chances of being eaten. Since cicadas are large and rich in protein, they are much-sought-after food for birds, small mammals and lizards. This dramatic flooding of the food market ensures that a larger proportion of the cicadas are able to survive, mate and lay eggs. It is quite simply a question of surviving by disappearing in the crowd. Since the time interval is so long, it is hardly likely that any predator will be able to adapt to it. And it is far from random that 13 and 17 are both prime numbers (numbers that can only be divided by themselves and 1). This means that a predator with a shorter cycle will never be 'in sync' with the cicada boom cycle. Having a cycle that involves a pretty large prime number therefore reduces the chances of being eaten. This really is a fairly impressive maths trick from an insect with the arithmetical ability of a toaster.

But how does the 17-year cicada know when it's time to put down its long drink and prepare to join the party on the surface? The trigger for their synchronised appearance is soil temperature. When the soil at depths of 20–30 centimetres has remained above 18°C for four days for the 17th time, the cicadas' internal alarm clocks all go off simultaneously. But we don't know quite how the countdown to year 17 happens. Part of the explanation appears to be a biological clock in which chemical compounds alter over time. Perhaps external signals from the tree also play a role, with the cicadas 'counting' the number of times it blossoms. Scientists who manipulated trees to blossom twice in one year did, in fact, find that 17-year cicadas emerged a year early.

There are singing cicadas in Europe, too, but they are not cyclical. Many people confuse cicadas (which are true bugs, order Hemiptera) with crickets and other grasshopper-like insects (which belong to the order Orthoptera, *see page 34*). Many of these also make a noise, but in different ways and at different times. The surging, intense insect sound you hear in the middle of a hot sunny day in southern Europe is typically the cicada.

Have you ever noticed those little 'spitballs' in the grass in summer? In many places, these spots of foam are known as 'cuckoo spit', although they have nothing to do with birds. However, inside the protective foam lies a little meadow spittlebug – a distant cousin of the Americans' fat 17-year cicadas. Our European spittlebugs, which do not sing, spend the whole of their childhood at a foam party. The foam is created when the cicada nymph blows air through some slime it excretes from its rectum. This protects it against both predators and dehydration.

Why Do Zebras Have Stripes?

We can blame or praise insects for many things and zebras' stripes may be among them. Because in the same way insects have evolved to deceive predators and trick victims, larger animals have evolved in response to irritating insects. Actually, the mystery of these stripes has plagued biologists since Darwin's days. Why in the world are these particular animals striped when the same types of animal elsewhere are not? Scores of creative theories have been proposed over the years. Might the stripes

provide camouflage for the animals when they are standing among small, scattered trees that cast a shadow?
Maybe the pattern confuses predators, so they can't quite
see where one zebra ends and the next one begins? Might
the stripes have a cooling effect because the air warms
up more rapidly over the black than the white sections,
thereby creating tiny eddies of air? Or could the stripes
serve a similar purpose to a conference name badge, letting the zebras know who's who?

This stripy debate hasn't yet been resolved, but some
recent research rejects all these suggestions in favour of a
fifth theory: the stripes repel insects.

Many infection-bearing insects live in the zebra's habitat,
including tsetse flies and other kinds of biting flies that
transmit diseases to large mammals. But if you are stripy,
you get off lightly. Infection bearers don't like landing on
striped surfaces. Why? Because stripes apparently confuse
the insects' visual orientation, especially when the zebras
are moving. The stripes create a kind of optical illusion,
like the way we humans may perceive the rotation of a
spoked wheel or propeller as different from its actual
rotation. So, the new theory is that evolution has promoted
the zebra's stripes because they lead to less insect trouble
and, consequently, improved survival rates.

By the way, have you ever wondered what colour the
zebra is beneath its stripes? Well, its skin is not striped,

it is black. In other words, the zebra is black with white stripes and not vice versa – there's a handy piece of trivia for your next pub quiz.

Insects as Guardians of Law and Order

Insects are staple food for birds, fish and many mammals. At the same time, we know that insects often eat each other, and this is absolutely crucial for keeping down the populations of what we think of as troublesome pests.

We know that an agricultural landscape where the fields are interspersed with varied flora provides a habitat for many of the pests' natural enemies. Similarly, woodland consisting of natural forest contains more predatory insects and parasites that keep spruce bark beetles and other pests in check than managed forests. Predatory insects and parasites control the amount of other small creatures in the forest. Swedish studies have found that the great spruce bark beetle – a species that can cause major damage to timber – has a great many more enemies in a natural forest with a variety of dead wood than in our normal, intensively managed forests.

In the garden, too, insects help to keep things in order. Take the wasp, for example. A growing wasps nest requires a lot of nourishment. It is said that a wasp can eat and eliminate a kilogram of other insects from a garden measuring a couple of hundred square metres – although the source of this claim is uncertain.

When it comes to spiders, however, we have fresh estimates of how much insect meat the massed spiders of the world actually devour in a year. And it is far from trifling: the planet's eight-legged insect relatives gobble down between 400 and 800 billion tonnes of insects a year. That's more meat than the entire human population manages to polish off even if we also factor in fish consumption.

To put it another way, the spiders of the planet could eat up every human being on Earth in a single year and still have room for more. Fortunately for us, they prefer to feast on the Earth's many insects instead.

CHAPTER 4

Insects and Plants:
A Never-ending Race

Although many insects are predators or parasites, most of them eat a plant diet – in the form of either salad (living plants) or compost (dead plants – discover more in Chapter 6, *page 134*).

There are many nuances to the salad diet: insects may eat nectar and pollen, seeds or the plant itself. There may also be some advantages in this for the plant, such as pollination or the dispersal of seeds. Over 120 million years, insects and plants developed tightly in tandem. They are often mutually dependent, but at the same time it is a never-ending race in which each party is out to secure more advantages for its own side. This love-hate relationship has led to some most peculiar forms of coexistence.

Drinking Crocodile Tears

The life of a herbivorous insect is no bed of roses! Plant tissue in general is pretty meagre fare, low on vital substances such as nitrogen and sodium. For instance, while the dry weight of most insects is at least 10 per cent nitrogen (sometimes much more, *see page 99*), plants overall contain only around 2–4 per cent. This has a number of consequences for herbivorous insects. Many have a lengthy larval period to ensure that they can acquire enough nourishment before metamorphosing and facing the adult world. Other larvae (with a shorter larval period) concentrate on the most nutritious parts of plants, such as the roots (where some plants have tenant bacteria that capture nitrogen for them) or the flowers and seeds. By the way, this is exactly what we humans do too – think of our staple foods like cereals and pulses.

Many aphid-like insects, which subsist by supping nitrogen-poor plant sap, have to guzzle up massive amounts – relative to their small size – to get enough nutrition. This leads to a tremendous surplus of water and sugar, which they excrete in the form of what we often call honeydew – much to the delight of other creatures (*see page 112*).

Plants also contain very little sodium, a substance that is crucial to the functioning of all creatures' muscles and nerve systems, among others. While members of the deer family, all herbivores, can acquire sodium by licking salt stones set out for them by friendly humans, insects must find natural sources that are rich in sodium. That is why you often see colourful butterflies sitting around a puddle, slurping up mineral-rich mud as a supplement to their nectar-based diet.

And if you can't find a puddle, how about crocodile tears? In 2013, fascinated field biologists on a trip down-river in the jungles of Costa Rica were able to film and photograph a beautiful orange butterfly and a bee drinking the tears of a caiman – a member of the crocodile family – each sipping from one of its eyes. It turns out that this method of acquiring vital salts from reptile tears is more widespread than we had thought, it is just rarely witnessed. Drinking crocodile tears undoubtedly sounds a bit more spectacular than slurping up puddles!

Willow: The Most Important Meal of the Spring

Pollination is a win-win activity that binds insects and plants together. The insect gets food in the form of sweet nectar or protein-rich pollen; the plants get their pollen moved from one flower to another, enabling fertilisation and the development of new seeds. Although some plants rely on the wind for cross-pollination or are self-pollinating, as many as eight out of 10 wild plants benefit from insect visits to their flowers.

Some plants are especially significant 'insect restaurants' because they supply nectar at a critical moment. The willow tree is one example. Normally, it lives a pretty anonymous existence out in forest and farmland. But in the spring, the willow enjoys its 15 minutes of fame. Because this is when the bumblebee queen comes tumbling out of her underground bedroom, where she has lain like Sleeping Beauty since the previous autumn. And she is hungry – after all, she hasn't eaten anything all winter. But there's no one around to prepare a delicious breakfast for her. Not yet. All the worker bumblebees called it a day when the autumn chill arrived, along with the previous year's queen, and now it's up to this queen to start a new community. If she is successful, both she and we humans will eventually end up with food on the table. Because bumblebees, wild bees and other insects are, as we know, crucial for the pollination of our food crops (about which more in Chapter 5, *page 104*). First, though, Her Royal Highness must find something to eat. And this is where the willow tree comes in, serving as nature's starting motor.

The willow doesn't hang about once the snow is melting on the hillsides. At a time when the other trees and plants have barely started to consider what to wear this year, the willow is already fully dressed. A bit lightly clad, admittedly, because the leaves won't arrive for some time. But the flowers are what matter here, during the first trysts of spring. The male and female flowers blossom on their separate trees: the male flowers are the familiar soft, grey catkins known in Norwegian as 'goslings', which eventually turn bright yellow, thanks to their pollen-bearing anthers; the female flowers are more discreet but contain more nectar than their male counterparts.

And this is the queen bumblebee's great stroke of luck: a fortifying breakfast that combines protein-rich pollen with a strengthening source of sugar nectar, all served up in the willow trees. This provides the energy that is urgently needed when you're about to set up a whole new community of pollinators single-handedly.

Once the bumblebee queen has eaten her fill, she will find a suitable nest site, either underground or above ground depending on·the species. Here, she will gather a ball of pollen in which to lay her first batch of eggs, before covering the ball with wax. Later, the newly hatched larvae will eat their way through this pollen-stuffed nursery. In the meantime, the queen is not being idle – she also builds a wax honey pot and fills it with regurgitated nectar. In this way she makes sure she can feed herself while incubating her eggs. Bumblebee eggs need to be kept at around 30°C to develop properly and the queen broods her eggs just as birds do. The queen actually has a bare spot on her abdomen to help disseminate the heat from her body to the eggs. In this first period she must sometimes leave the nest for short foraging trips, but as the colony grows, the workers take over the gathering of pollen and nectar and the queen concentrates on laying eggs.

Later in summer, the bumblebee queen stops producing female workers. Instead, she lays unfertilised eggs that develop into males, and the larvae from her fertilised eggs are now fed in a way that makes them develop into new queens. With autumn drawing close, the new queens and the males mate. For the old queen, the males and the rest of the summer's colony, it's game over. Only the new, now-mated queen survives and crawls into a cosy space underground, ready for a long sleep, until spring awakens and the cycle begins again.

Globeflower: Nature's Bed and Breakfast

Coupledom can be complicated, and that applies to the pollinating relationship between insects and plants too. The pollination of the globeflower is a case in point. With its bright yellow, almost closed head, the globeflower is easy to spot in meadow and waterside locations in the United Kingdom, but not so easy to access.

Only three or four insect species, all belonging to a family known as globeflower flies, are able to find their way into this tightly packed miniature sun of a flower. But they are amply rewarded: it turns out that the globeflower is a bit like a bed and breakfast, offering its visitors a hearty meal!

The globeflower provides the very best it has to offer: its own seeds. I'm not sure whether they contain as much protein as bacon and eggs, but they must certainly taste pretty good to an exhausted fly. Strictly speaking, the adult flies aren't the ones helping themselves to the grub, either – they just lay eggs in the ovules inside the flower, and that's where the larvae grow up. In fact, the only place they are able to develop is inside a globeflower seed.

So, how in the world do globeflowers organise things so that a steady stream of flies can move from flower to flower with pollen? It's a question of collaboration and an ingenious balance between flower and fly. Because these particular flies are the only ones that can pollinate the globeflower, without their visits there would be no globe-flower babies – in other words, no seeds. No wonder the flowers bend over backwards to offer the very best they have at their disposal. Yet it is an incredibly fine balancing act. If the flies eat up all the seeds, there will be no more globeflowers, and over the long term that means there will no longer be any hosts offering board and lodging – and this in turn means no more new flies either, so it is crucial for the flies to lay eggs in a suitable proportion of the seeds.

Quite how the flies work that out remains an open question, but the fact is, it works.

An Innocent Pizza Herb? Far From It!

Oregano is another example of complex interaction between plants and insects because this green herb, much used in Italian cuisine, is party to a cunning intrigue involving powerful alliances, disguises and forgery.

Picture an arid, sun-drenched hillside in northern Italy emanating a heady scent of oregano, thyme and marjoram. One of the oregano plants feels a tickling sensation around its nether regions: a bunch of *Myrmica* ants have decided to set up their nest beside the plant's roots. Now and then they gobble up a few small roots as they go about their work. This is hardly beneficial for the plant, which responds to the ants' munching by upping its production of carvacrol, a substance that defends it against insects. Most ants have zero tolerance for the insecticide, but this particular species has learnt to cope with it and stands its ground down there among the roots. We humans prize this defensive substance: carvacrol is what gives oregano its intense herbal scent. But the aromatic substance has several functions. In Italian flower meadows, it also serves as an SOS, a kind of shout in the language of scent directed at a totally different species. The recipient is a beautiful butterfly known as the Large Blue. It lays its eggs on the plant and the larva then spends a couple of weeks there, developing and simultaneously preparing a disguise that would be the envy of any undercover agent. We're not talking false moustaches and hair dye here, because the visual aspect isn't especially important for ants. Scent is, however, which is why the butterfly larva veils itself in an alluring cloak of ant scent, perfectly adapted to the aroma of the ants living beneath the flower.

Next comes a critical moment: the larva lets go of the plant and tumbles to the ground. A *Myrmica* ant comes toddling by on its way home from the eternal round of food gathering. It finds the butterfly larva, is tricked by the scent into thinking it's a larva from the ants' nest and carefully carries the butterfly larva into the darkness of the nest, where it is adopted on the spot. Even though it differs from the ant offspring in both size and colour, it is nursed, cared for and fed on regurgitated food by adult worker ants, who tend to it as diligently as they care for the nest's own young. But the butterfly larva, which needs to multiply its weight by several hundred per cent before it's done, is not content with recycled sugar water. As soon as its adoptive mothers turn their backs, the greedy butterfly larva tucks into the nest's stock of ant larvae. It supplements its aromatic disguise by imitating the sounds made by the ant queen – a kind of clicking song. This convinces the workers that the butterfly larva is a high-ranking ant and so none of them intervene while it runs amok in the nursery.

By the end, the butterfly larva has more or less polished off the entire colony. Peace returns to the area around the oregano plant's roots and the larva can pupate. If it isn't reared in the right kind of ants' nest, the butterfly has no chance of producing future generations. Who'd have thought so much drama lay behind that scattering of green herbs on your pizza?

Seeds Play a Crappy Trick on Dung Beetles

In the case of oregano, both the plant and the butterfly benefited from the collaboration, but sometimes one of the parties has the upper hand and 'tricks' the other. Like when the red-tailed robber bumblebee *Bombus wurflenii* can't be bothered to crawl past the stamen buried in Northern Wolfsbane flowers to get to the nectar. Instead, it takes a shortcut, simply biting through the flower head and helping itself to the good stuff, having done nothing whatsoever to earn it. Because that way, there won't be any pollination.

Other times, the plant draws the long straw, as in the case of the reed-like *Ceratocaryum argenteum*, which only grows in South Africa. Cleverly enough, it produces seeds that look like dung: big, round dark-brown lumps identical in appearance to the leavings of the local antelopes.

Just as some clothing chains pre-perfume the garments they sell, this plant ensures that its 'sales products' – the seeds – have an attractive scent too: the scent of dung. Because it is targeting a very particular group of customers.

Normally, it's daft for seeds to have a strong smell since that makes it easier for hungry little seed-eating creatures to find and eat them. The explanation for this mystery came as a surprise. It was discovered by a group of scientists from Cape Town University who were actually supposed to be researching whether small rodents ate these strange heavy seeds. They set out nearly 200 *Ceratocaryum* seeds in a nature reserve in South Africa, sort of like free samples. And, as in the human world, the whole thing had to be documented photographically, of course, so motion-sensitive cameras were set up beside all the seeds.

It turned out that the seeds were removed not by rodents in search of food but by gullible dung beetles who fell hook, line and sinker for the seeds' advertising offensive. These beetles believed the smelly balls were antelope dung of the type they bury and then lay their eggs in.

Incidentally, dung beetles perform an extremely important service to the ecosystem by burying genuine animal muck, as this prevents pastureland from drowning in dung, and ensures that the nutrients return to the soil (*see pages*

155 and 163). In this case, though, the beetles were tricked: they trustingly trundled away the spherical dung-like seeds and buried them a couple of centimetres beneath the earth. At least a quarter of the seeds were sown in a new location – job done!

And what did the dung beetles get for their labour? Nothing. The scientists hid in the bushes and dug up the seeds as soon as the mother beetle had shuffled off. They found no sign of eggs and no trace of any attempt to eat the seed either. Apparently, the beetles ultimately discovered that they had been tricked and gave the whole thing up as a bad job. If beetles were capable of blushing, perhaps we would have seen the beetle mother's cheeks burn red when her naivety was exposed live on camera. Imagine being taken in by a reed – a pretty mean trick!

Seeds That Serve Up a Packed Lunch for Ants

There are plenty of other plants that get insects, mostly ants, to disperse their seeds for them in return for a reward. We know of this in more than 11,000 different plants, or almost 5 per cent of all plant species. It is common for the plant to ensure that there is some sort of payment in the form of a valuable supplement: a packed lunch for the ant. The ant carries the whole thing home to the anthill, but while the packed lunch is being served up to the hungry ant babies, the seed is thrown away, generally beneath the earth in or near the anthill. Some of the seeds are also lost in transit.

In the United Kingdom, too, ants help many plants, including common cow wheat, violets and wood anemone. One cunning adaptation may be for plants to flower and produce seeds early, before the ants have much else worth eating, as this increases the chance of getting help with transport. The next time you see a common hepatica in spring, take a closer look when the flowers fall off and you'll see the little white ant packed lunches sitting on each seed.

Other plants have taken the collaboration with ants a step further, not just serving up food but also building the ants a house. Acacias are the classic example: some develop enlarged thorns where the ants can live, and provide them with nutritious food in the form of small packets of oils and proteins. In return, the ants keep peckish herbivores at bay and graze on competing vegetation around the acacias.

Wood Wide Web – Underground Internet for Plants

Collaboration may be the smartest option when insects are on the warpath. And here, plants are helped by an entirely different species: fungi. There's a lot more to the chanterelle or porcini mushroom than the cap that catches your eye while you're out mushrooming in the autumn. A large part of these mushrooms is hidden beneath the forest soil, forming the wood's concealed communication system – a network of fungal threads that links trees and plants, allowing them to communicate. Yes, *communicate*. We are constantly learning more about this close collaboration between fungi and roots, known as *mycorrhiza* (literally 'fungus roots'), which we actually find in 90 per cent of all the plants on Earth.

One thing this relationship does is help plants grow, as the fungus transfers water and plant nutrition from the soil. We have known about that for a long time. But the fungal network can also be used to send messages – about an insect attack, for example. Just like a school sending emails to all parents when the school nurse finds head lice in Class 6b, or the public health institute issuing an internet warning about the onset of this year's influenza bug, a plant attacked by insects can send chemical signals via the subterranean internet to say: 'Watch out, here come the aphids again!'

In an ingeniously constructed study, British scientists planted beans and allowed some of the plants to develop fungus roots but stopped others from doing so. Next, they eliminated the possibility of sending signals through the air by wrapping the plants in special bags that prevented signalling molecules from getting through. The next step was to let aphids loose on certain plants. According to the scientists' findings, plants that didn't get chewed themselves but *did* have contact with the plants under attack via the fungal internet developed defensive substances to protect them against the aphid attack; the isolated plants did not.

In forests, trees also use this underground internet – call it the Wood Wide Web, if you will – to send each other carbon. Some scientists think that the oldest and largest trees in the forest, 'the mother trees', help the young saplings in the early phase of their lives by sending a kind of food parcel through the network. Even trees of different species may send each other nutrition in this way. Perhaps we need to reconsider the way we think about forests: individual trees may be more closely linked than we had realised.

Working Your Land

Agriculture and animal husbandry are the basis of our modern civilisation. They have permitted high population density, with all the opportunities that entails, but we humans were pitifully late starters compared to insects. Our agricultural revolution only happened 10,000 years ago. By then, ants and termites had already been practising agriculture for 50 million years and ants had been keeping livestock for twice as long. Is it any wonder that ants beat us hands down when it comes to the number of individuals on the planet, and that the combined weight of these minute but multitudinous six-legged creatures matches the weight of all the human beings on Earth?

Insects don't grow plants – they grow fungi. Specially adapted fungi that only grow in the ants' fields, in the same way as our crop plants have adapted to a life 'in captivity'. In South and Central America, leaf-cutter ants are common. Long columns of workers trudge off to cut off suitably sized sections of leaves and bring them back to the nest beneath the earth. The machinery that then takes over is so well oiled that it would exceed the wildest dreams of any industrial magnate. A long column of ants, all of slightly differing sizes, do exactly what is needed – without demanding longer lunch breaks, better shifts, or an end to zero-hour contracts.

The leaves are chewed up and distributed across the 'kitchen garden'. Other, smaller ants lick the fresh mass of leaves, thereby transferring fungi from the established parts of the garden. Even smaller ants shuffle carefully around in the garden, removing 'weeds', which in this case means bacteria or the wrong kinds of fungus. Once the fungus has grown and spread across the new section of the garden, certain ants work to harvest the nutrient-rich parts of the fungus and send the candy-floss-like food around to all the rest, including the growing generation of ant larvae.

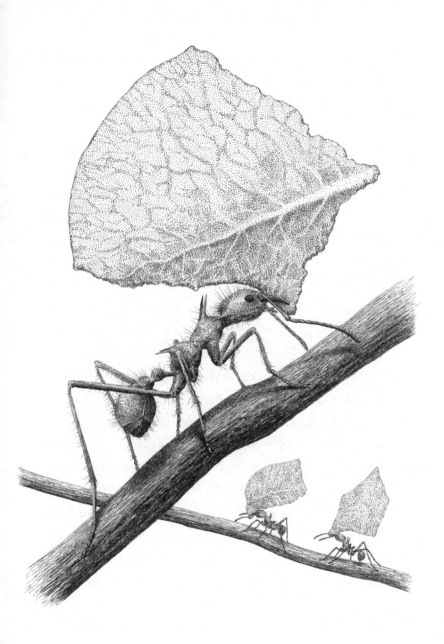

As in a well-run factory, this sort of streamlined production requires good access to raw materials. In the course of a year, an average leaf-cutter ant colony clears and maintains 2.7 kilometres of ant paths, radiating out from the colony like the spokes of a bicycle wheel.

The agriculture practised by termites resembles that of the leaf-cutter ants, but in this case the nest is built of earth and wood pulp mixed with spit, and lies partly beneath and partly above the ground. A sophisticated air-conditioning system ensures that the temperature is maintained at optimal levels in the subterranean fungus gardens (*see page 193*). And termites don't bring in green leaves: they carry home sticks, grass and straw. With the aid of their fungus partner, the plant matter is broken down and converted into more digestible termite food. The two parties, termite and fungus, are dependent on one another.

Certain bark beetles that live in wood also rely on fungus. This enables them to convert cellulose into edible material. These ambrosia beetles, as they're called, pretty much take a dinner-in-a-box kit with them when they move into a newly dead tree: they have special cavities in their body (mycangia), where they store a certain type of fungus. Once installed in their new accommodation, a dying or newly dead tree, they're not content just to lay eggs in a crack; no, they excavate splendid chambers and corridors beneath the bark and there they plant the fungus that will be grown as in a kind of allotment to provide healthy, nourishing food for the beetle babies. And this is probably necessary, since the beetles' family life is not quite like our own. After the beetle mum lays her eggs, she does a runner, leaving the kids to butter their own bread, so it's a good thing she has at least taken the trouble to fill the pantry before leaving!

We don't know how ants and termites manage to maintain high, stable production, even in such an extreme monoculture where they cultivate only a single species. It would be good news for our own future food production if we could wheedle this secret out of the insects.

Aphids as Dairy Cattle

Ants' animal husbandry is no less impressive. As described earlier (*see page 98*), aphids produce large amounts of sweet surplus liquid and some ant species provide bodyguard services in return for this substance. For the ants, easy access to carbohydrates is so attractive that they happily, and aggressively, defend their herd of 'sugar cows' against anything that might even think of eating them. An ant colony can easily harvest 10–15 kilograms of sugar from aphids over a summer; some estimates go as high as 100 kilograms of sugar per anthill per year.

Ants have also been found to 'herd' their cattle by

restricting the aphids' capacity to disperse to other plants. Just as we humans clip the wings of geese and other winged livestock, ants may bite the wings off aphids. They can also use signalling chemicals to prevent the development of winged individuals or limit how far the aphids stray on foot.

The ants' nurturing of these sap-sucking insects can be a disadvantage for the host plant – hardly surprising, perhaps, since aphids and their relatives hoover up huge amounts of plant sap. Some American scientists found proof of this when they were actually supposed to be studying the co-dependent relationship between ants and tiny cicada-like insects called treehoppers on the yellow rabbit-brush shrub out in the field in Colorado. To their irritation, black bears kept turning up and destroying the ant nests in some of the areas they planned to study (taking a chunk out of the field equipment along the way).

In the end, the scientists decided to shift their focus and look at how the bear influenced the system instead. They then discovered that the plants grew better where the bear was present, owing to a sophisticated domino effect. When the bear ate the ants, there were fewer ants to frighten off the ladybirds. That meant there were more ladybirds. Since these were now left to eat in peace, they helped themselves to the treehoppers and other herbivores. As a result, there were fewer bothersome insects on the plant, which therefore grew better. That is how the presence of bears can improve plant growth – by keeping the ants in check!

Small Creatures, Great Significance

Connections don't always work the way we think they do. One example of this stems from the wheat fields in the arid parts of Australia. In this case scientists wanted to study the positive contribution of insects, especially ants and termites, so they compared the wheat harvest in fields where these insects had been eliminated by insecticide and fields where ants and termites were allowed to remain.

It turned out that the wheat harvest rose 36 per cent where crops had *not* been sprayed. Why? In areas as arid as this, there are no earthworms, so ants and termites do the earthworm's job instead, creating corridors that allow more water to trickle down into the soil. The water content was twice as high in the soil where these insects were allowed to live as in the soil where they had been eliminated. In addition, the nitrogen content was much higher. This may be because termites' guts contain bacteria that capture nitrogen from the air. And as if it wasn't already enough that the insects improved the soil's supply of water and nutrients – seed-eating ants also ensured that there were only half as many weeds in the unsprayed fields as in the sprayed fields.

But there's no need to travel halfway across the planet to

see the significance of ants. We can find other examples in Europe, right outside our own back door. A Swedish study of coniferous forests shows how tiny ants might affect massive issues, like the climate, by influencing carbon storage in forests.

Take a walk in any woodland around your way and find yourself an anthill. This is the home of wood ants – hill-building ants of the *Formica* genus. In an experiment conducted in northern Sweden, scientists excluded these ants from small areas of the forest floor with major consequences.

First, the entire community changed. The four most common herbs became even more common. This increased the supply of nutrients to the soil in the forest because woodland herbs like cow wheat and *Linnaea borealis*, or twin flower decompose more easily than woody berry shrubs. The increase in nutrients was like putting a rocket under the tiny caretakers of the woodland soil. Most notably, the activity of various bacteria increased. This also led to the decomposition of old and seasoned remnants of dead plants.

So, what was the net result of keeping wood ants at bay? Well, because the changes in the decomposition community meant that old, stored carbon was now suddenly being broken down, the scientists observed an overall 15 per cent *decline* in the forest soil's storage of carbon and nitrogen. If this result holds true when scaled up, it means that in the absence of ants, a substantial proportion of the large carbon stock in boreal forest soil would be lost. Bearing in mind that northern forests cover 11 per cent of the Earth's surface and store more carbon than any other type of woodland, it is clear that, despite their modest size, the wood ants have a major influence on fundamental processes such as the circulation of nutrients and carbon storage.

A Troublesome Cactus

We humans have long exploited the close relationship between insects and plants, and between predatory and herbivorous insects. Ancient Chinese documents, apparently from around the year 300 BCE, tell farmers how to move the papery nests of a certain ant into the lemon groves to reduce the pests on the lemons. It was also common to set up bamboo 'suspension bridges' between the trees to make it easier for the ants to move from tree to tree and keep away the pests. This appears to be one of the first examples of what we call biological control – the use of living organisms in the battle against pests, as an alternative to using chemicals.

We have moved species from one end of the planet to another, often quite intentionally, and with extremely variable results. Sometimes, things have gone terribly wrong.

Like in Australia in the 1800s, when somebody had the bright idea of setting up production of cochineal dye (*see page 183*) and optimistically imported a few shiploads of prickly pears from Mexico. The cochineal production went down the drain but the prickly pears spread like wildfire. By 1900, the cactuses covered an area the size of Denmark. Just 20 years later, the area was six times larger. A region the size of Great Britain was totally unusable for grazing or crop growing because it was overgrown by spiky cactuses. It was a crisis. The authorities offered a generous reward to anybody who could come up with a way of combating the prickly pears – the reward was never claimed.

In the end, one World War and much desperation later, the solution arrived – in the form of an insect from South America. An anonymous moth-like Lepidopteran of the *Cactoblastis* genus, whose larvae chew passageways through prickly pears, was brought in, tested and bred in massive numbers. A hundred men in seven lorries drove around the whole of Queensland and New South Wales, handing out paper quills filled with *Cactoblastis* eggs to the landowners. In the five years from 1926 to 1931, more than two billion eggs were distributed.

It was a spectacular success. By as early as 1932, the moth larvae had killed off the cactuses in large parts of the fallow land. This is still one of the prime examples of successful biological control.

But there's always another side to the coin. After the success in Australia, the moth was used to biologically control cactuses in several other places, including the Caribbean islands. From there, *Cactoblastis* moths have spread to Florida, where they now threaten to wipe out unique local cactuses.

CHAPTER 5

Busy Flies, Flavoursome Bugs:
Insects and Our Food

S o, you say you don't like insects? Well, then – maybe
you don't like chocolate, marzipan, apples or strawberries either. The fact is that these and countless other
foodstuffs can only be produced in the quantities and quality to which we are accustomed with the help of insects.
What we are talking about here, of course, is insects' work
in the field of pollination.

Insect visits to flowers contribute to seed production in
more than 80 per cent of the world's wild plants, and insect
pollination improves fruit or seed quality or quantity in
a large proportion of our global food crops. Although
wind-pollinated crops (such as rice, corn and various other
grains) account for the majority of our energy intake,
insect-pollinated fruits, berries and nuts are important
energy boosters, as well as being a vital source of variety in

our diet. We know that the species richness of wild pollinating insects matters, too: a study of 40 different crops across the planet showed that visits from wild insects increased crop yields in all systems.

And we are cultivating a steadily increasing number of crops that require pollination – according to the Intergovernmental Science-Policy Platform on Biodiversity and Ecosystem Services (IPBES), the volume of such crops has tripled over the past 50 years – but the occurrence and species diversity of wild pollinating species is simultaneously declining.

Some pollination also results in a by-product, and one in particular that we all know and love is honey – a natural sweetener with a long history. And if you fancy supplementing your diet with a spot of environmentally friendly protein, why not eat the insects themselves? They're packed with nourishment and form part of a normal human diet in most areas of the world – except the West.

In this chapter, we'll take a closer look at insects' role in our food supply.

Sweet Stuff Steeped in History

We love sweet stuff! The UK's average per capita sugar consumption currently stands at around 35 kilos per year. This is hardly surprising because the difficulty we humans have in resisting a bowlful of sweets is deeply ingrained in us. Once upon a time our ape ancestors sprinted their shaggy way around Africa eating fruit. Since the sweetest, ripest fruit had the highest energy content, we gradually evolved a preference for sweetness. Back then, before the days of pick-and-mix counters, it simply made sense to have a sweet tooth.

Anybody who has ever accidentally left a banana in a gym bag knows that ripe fruit has an extremely short shelf life. But there is another source of sweetness that is much less perishable and has long been in use: honey. In 2003, construction work on Europe's second-longest oil pipeline unearthed honey jars in the 5,500-year-old grave of a woman in Georgia.

So, what exactly is honey? It is created when bees extract nectar from flowers, collecting it in a honey sac – a special pouch that lies between the oesophagus and the stomach. This prevents the nectar that will later become honey from mingling with the food passing through the bees' digestive system. Once inside the honey sac, the nectar mixes with the bees' enzymes. When the bees return to the hive, they regurgitate the contents of their sac, passing it on to other bees, who store it in their own honey sacs, transport it further into the hive and regurgitate it into the mouths of yet more bees. In the end, the honey is stored in wax cells, where it remains for later use – or until we humans harvest it.

Hallucinogenic Honey

In the Spider Cave (Cuevas de la Araña) in Valencia, Spain, 8,000-year-old cave paintings depict the harvesting of wild honey. They show a man dangling from a rope or vine surrounded by swarming bees, one hand holding a collecting basket and the other inside the nest.

In Asia, vestiges of bee- and honey-based cultures still persist in the food as well as the culture and economy. Twice a year the honey hunters in the foothills of the Himalayas harvest the honey of the Himalayan giant honeybee (*Apis dorsata laboriosa*), the world's largest honeybee. It is a hazardous venture, which involves climbing up high cliffs using ladders and ropes amid the buzz of cantankerous bees. These days, pressure from tourists keen to witness the phenomenon is causing over-harvesting of the bee colonies; at the same time, erosion and the shrinkage of wilderness areas are altering the surrounding landscape, all of which are having adverse consequences for the bees. Furthermore, it did little to diminish attention levels when journalists discovered that one variant of the honey gathered in the mountains of Nepal had hallucinogenic properties. The reason for this is that the bees gather poisonous nectar from plants such as rhododendrons and bog rosemary or related heather plants. As a result, the honey may contain a poison called grayanotoxin, which not only affects your pulse and makes you dizzy and nauseous, but can also cause hallucinations.

In fact, 'mad honey' is a recognised phenomenon even in Europe. Accounts from antiquity tell of a disastrous military campaign in around 400 BCE, during which thousands of Greek soldiers retreating through present-day Turkey helped themselves to some wild honey. Despite the absence of enemies, their camp soon resembled a battlefield. According to the Ancient Greek military commander and writer Xenophon, the soldiers raved like drunkards, quite out of their wits. Diarrhoea and vomiting rampaged through the camp and only some days later were the men fit enough to struggle to their feet and resume their homeward march.

Other sources from antiquity describe the use of hallucinogenic honey as a weapon of war. A few wax honeycombs of rhododendron honey are ever so casually placed in the enemy's path – for who can resist a spot of the sweet stuff when they happen to stumble across it? The intoxicated soldiers are then easy to pick off.

This kind of honey is still produced in parts of Turkey, where it is known as *deli bal*. But there's no need to worry about poisoning yourself by eating 'mad honey'. Fortunately, it's rare for the concentration in the modern, commercially produced honey to be high enough to have ill effects.

Beyond that, honey has long been prized for its anti-bacterial properties. Historically, it was used on wounds, and it is said that when Alexander the Great died in Babylon, aged just 33, he was submerged in a honey-filled coffin to preserve his body over the two years it would take to transport him to his burial place in Alexandria. The truth of this story is difficult to establish.

The Sweet Taste of Teamwork

One story that is certainly true, however, despite sounding pretty incredible, is the tale of a bird called the greater honeyguide (with the apt Latin name *Indicator indicator*). This African species helps us humans to find honey. The honeyguide is fond of both honey and wax and wouldn't say no to a smattering of bee larvae either, and is famous for its unique behaviour. As the name suggests, it can tell other animals and humans where to find honey. In return, it counts on receiving a share in the booty once the nest is broken up by something larger and stronger than itself.

Whereas most birds fly away on our approach, the opposite happens with the honeyguide. It seeks out humans, twitters, and then flies a little way off to see if they're following. New research has shown that the birds respond to certain human sounds. The Yao are a tribe in Mozambique who still find honey in collaboration with the honeyguide. When the scientists played recordings of the Yao people's special calls aloud, this increased both the probability that the honeyguide would appear and the probability of it leading them to the bee's nest. The overall probability of finding honey rose from 16 to 54 per cent. This is one of very few examples of mutual, active collaboration between wild animals and humans.

We have known of this peculiar collaboration since the 1500s, but some anthropologists think it may go all the way back to the days of *Homo erectus*. In that case, we're talking 1.8 million years. That tells you a bit about how sought-after this product of the insect world has been for both animals and human beings for thousands of years.

Manna, the Miracle Food

Insects have other sweet titbits to offer too. And they could well be the origin of manna, the miracle food mentioned in the Bible – unless we think of it as a purely miraculous product, that is. According to the Old Testament, manna was the food the Israelites survived on during their journey from Egypt to Israel. This was something of a trip: a 40-year expedition through the barren Sinai Peninsula with few opportunities to lay their hands on food.

That precise thought also struck the Israelites: 'And the children of Israel said to them, "Oh, that we had died by the hand of the Lord in the land of Egypt, when we sat by the pots of meat and when we ate bread to the full! For you have brought us out into this wilderness to kill this whole assembly with hunger".'

But the Lord, who had already taken care to equip the world with 'everything that creeps on the Earth' in the Book of Genesis, had a solution: '"Behold, I will rain bread from heaven for you." And when the layer of dew lifted, there, on the surface of the wilderness, was a small round substance, as fine as frost on the ground. So when the children of Israel saw it, they said to one another, "What is it?" For they did not know what it was. And Moses said to them, "This is the bread which the Lord has given you to eat." And the house of Israel called its name Manna. And it was like white coriander seed, and the taste of it was like wafers made with honey. And the children of Israel ate manna for forty years, until they came to an inhabited land.' (All quotations from *Exodus 16*, New King James Version of the Bible.)

A slightly monotonous diet perhaps: 40 years of nothing but honey wafers would be enough to cure the sweetest tooth. However, it seems to have been satisfactory hiking food because the Israelites did reach their destination, after all. But are there any natural edible products in this part of the world that might have inspired the description of manna, the miracle food?

Proposed answers, with varying degrees of probability, range from the sap of various bushes or trees, such as the manna ash (*Fraxinus ornus*), to hallucinogenic mushrooms (*Psilocybe cubensis*), fragments of lichen (manna lichen or *Lecanora esculenta*) or algae scum (*Spirulina*) carried by the wind, to mosquito larvae, tadpoles or other aquatic animals whisked away by tornadoes.

The strongest hypothesis is that manna may have been crystallised honeydew from a sap-sucking insect, specifically the Tamarisk manna scale (*Trabutina mannipara*). This little insect belongs to the scale insect family and sucks sap from the tamarisk tree (*Tamarix* genus), which grows extensively across the Middle East.

Because the sap sucked up by the manna scale (and many other sap-sucking insects, *see page 98*) is much heavier on sugar than nitrogen, the insects have to jettison the surplus sugar. They do this by excreting a sugary secretion called honeydew. Large quantities of the sweet substance can accumulate on the tamarisk trees and dry into sugar crystals. People in Iraq and other Arab countries still gather these lumps of sugar from tamarisk trees and consider them a delicacy.

If this is the origin of the biblical manna, we might imagine that the wind loosened the crystals and sprinkled them on the earth, making it appear that sugar crystals were raining from the heavens.

Marathon Food

Perhaps the Israelites ought to have taken some hornet juice with them on their long and arduous journey too. It has been shown that the larvae of an Asian hornet produce a substance that is nowadays marketed as a miracle product to boost sporting endurance and performance.

Adult hornets cannot eat solid protein. So instead, they fly home to the nest and feed their larvae small chunks of meat. The larvae have mouths with teeth in and can chomp away. In exchange for these chunks of meat, the larvae regurgitate a kind of jelly that the adults then slurp up.

Once people grasped that the contents of this jelly were crucial for the adult hornet's endurance – they can fly 100 kilometres a day at a speed of 40kph – it wasn't long before commercial products aimed at athletes came on the market. Do they work? Debatable. But they certainly sell. Especially since Japanese long-distance runner Naoko Takahashi won the Olympic gold medal for the women's marathon in Sydney in 2000 and gave much of the credit for her victory to the hornet extract. Sales really took off then! Today, you can buy sports drinks containing hornet larva extract in Japan, and similar products have also caught on in the US.

Billions of Starving Locusts

Sometimes insects simply eat our food. Locust swarms have been – and remain – a feared example of just that. In the Bible, swarms of locusts are described as one of the 10 plagues God inflicted upon Egypt.

> So Moses stretched out his rod over the land of Egypt, and the Lord brought an east wind on the land all that day and all that night. When it was morning, the east wind brought the locusts. And the locusts went up over all the land of Egypt and rested on all the territory of Egypt. They were very severe; previously there had been no such locusts as they, nor shall there be such after them. For they covered the face of the whole Earth, so that the land was darkened; and they ate every herb of the land and all the fruit of the trees which the hail had left.
>
> *Exodus 2: 10: 13–15,*
> New King James Version

One fascinating aspect of this biblical quotation is that it remains accurate to this day in strictly ecological terms. Only when the *khamsin*, a warm south-easterly wind, has blown for at least 24 hours can swarms of locusts reach Egypt from the areas where they originate further east.

And it is a truly terrible sight. A single locust can eat its own bodyweight in food every day. And once we grasp that a swarm can contain 10 billion of these starving, flying, jumping creatures, distributed over an area about the size of Liverpool, we begin to understand how the sky would be darkened, and why they left not a single stalk of grass behind them.

Locust swarms still appear at irregular intervals, mainly in Africa and the Middle East, although estimations indicate swarms are capable of affecting up to 20 per cent of the Earth's land surface. The mechanism behind locust plagues is like a one-way version of Dr Jekyll and Mr Hyde. Normally, the locust is a nice and shy creature, and does not cause any harm to crops. But when special weather conditions make their numbers surge, space becomes tight and they repeatedly bump into each other, which triggers a hormone that changes both the way they look and the way they behave, in a matter of hours. They grow bigger, darker and hungrier, and all of a sudden feel strongly attracted to one another. Large bands of restless locusts form, moving across the landscape and meeting up with other bands to form even bigger groups. One theory is that starvation can lead to cannibalism in locusts and that the swarming behaviour has evolved as an alternative.

Yet the fact that insects eat plants we ourselves want to eat is not solely negative. Many food crops we prize for their acidic, bitter or strong taste have developed these flavours as a defence against grazing, by insects among other creatures. Think of herbs like oregano (*see page 86*), or the peppermint tea you're so fond of, or the mustard you squeeze on your hotdog. If the plants no longer needed a defence, they would spare their resources for other purposes and the taste might change. Many of the active ingredients in medicines extracted from plants may have originated from the plants' need to avoid being eaten by insects and larger animals.

Chocolate's Tiny Best Chum

We humans love our chocolate! Worldwide consumption is steadily rising and Britons polish off more than 8 kilograms of the stuff a year. At the same time, producers now warn of a possible shortage in the near future, citing global causes such as climate change and increased consumption in countries like China and India. But there's actually one teensy-weensy factor nobody is discussing that is crucial to ensuring your access to chocolate; a little midge, in fact, smaller than the head of a pin. Friendless and nameless in English. But perhaps it isn't so easy to make friends when you're the size of a poppy seed and all your relatives are blood-sucking jerks. Because the midge in question belongs to the family of biting midges, those teeny insects known in the US as 'No-See-Ums' that crawl through your mosquito net and find their way into your ears and behind your glasses, and just can't resist a few drops of warm blood.

Despite all that, this tiny insect is almost single-handedly responsible for the coating on your digestives, the chocolate bar that sweetens your hike and the cup of cocoa that warms your bones on a chilly winter's day. Because out in the rainforests, this relative of the biting midge – the chocolate midge – has foregone blood in favour of a lifetime spent crawling in and out of cacao flowers.

These beautiful blossoms, which grow straight out of the stem of the cacao tree, are very intricately constructed. The chocolate midge is one of the few insects that can be bothered – and is small enough – to crawl into a cacao flower and get the pollination done.

But the romantic relationship between the cacao tree and the chocolate midge is complicated because it won't do to use pollen from another flower on the same tree: no, pollination requires the right stuff, from a neighbouring tree. If you consider that our new insect friend can barely carry enough pollen to pollinate a single flower, is bad at flying and that the flowers only last a day or two before falling off, you'll get an idea of just how tough this particular relationship is.

In addition, the chocolate midge has certain stipulations when it comes to the fittings in its home: it needs shade and high humidity, and a layer of rotten leaves on the floor of the nursery. This is because its larvae develop in humid compost on the floor of the rainforest.

So, this process doesn't produce a great deal of cacao – even less so when the growing is done in open plantations that are too dry and too far from the shade for the midge's liking. Only three out of 1,000 cacao flowers in plantations are successfully pollinated and go on to become mature fruit. On average, a cacao tree produces enough cacao beans for barely 5 kilograms of chocolate in its entire 25-year lifetime.

To convert that into a more recognisable currency, this means that three months' worth of the entire production of a single cacao tree is required to produce, say, a KitKat. Plus, the hard work of pollination done by hordes of industrious chocolate midges.

Marzipan's Midwife

Marzipan is simple: just take some finely ground almonds and icing sugar, and add a smidgeon of egg white to bind it all together. Yet marzipan owes its existence to a pretty complicated 'birth' that takes place in sunny California.

Eighty per cent of the world's almond production comes

from the Golden State, where the climate is ideally suited to intensive production so farmers exploit the area to the max. Long rows of almond trees cover an area roughly the size of Hampshire in the UK.

The almonds are harvested in September using a mechanical shaking machine that shakes every single tree to make the almonds tumble down. They are then left to lie on the ground for a few days to dry before being swept together and sucked up by an oversized vacuum cleaner that drives between the trees. And now we're getting to the root of the problem: ideally, there should be nothing between the almond trees but bare, hard-packed earth as this improves both efficiency and almond hygiene. However, it also means that natural flower pollinators such as bees and other insects can find nothing to eat for miles around – pretty tricky considering that almond trees rely on pollination to produce almonds. This explains the massive moving operation that takes place in the US each February. Honeybees are needed on site, so more than a million beehives are transported on specially constructed trucks from all over the US, like some vast NATO exercise. More than half of all the country's beehives can be found in California every spring, just so you and I get to enjoy our marzipan.

So, the next time you're chomping on a chunk of marzipan, send a few friendly thoughts in the direction of the bees – marzipan's midwives.

Beans, Bees and Bowel Movements

Coffee has many functions. It can give you a boost during your break; the coffee machine is an indispensable hub of workplace socialising, and a cup of coffee is a crucial morning pick-me-up for many people, myself included.

Legend has it that an Ethiopian goatherd was the first person to discover the stimulating effect of coffee. He noticed that after eating the red coffee beans his usually grumpy goats began to gambol around joyfully – and so did he when he tried them himself. One day, a passing monk managed to work out the connection. Hey presto! He was suddenly able to stay awake through even the lengthiest prayer services.

Although this may not necessarily be the whole and unvarnished truth about the origin of coffee drinking, what *is* undeniable is that we are continually learning more about the role different animal species can play in ensuring that our beloved coffee finds its way to our cup. But we're talking here about animals that are considerably smaller – or a great deal larger – than a goat.

Let's start with the tiny insects. It seems that even though the most common coffee plant can sort out pollination for itself inside each flower, the coffee crop is much higher if the bushes exchange pollen. And since the coffee flower blossoms for an extremely short time, nothing works better than a grain of pollen delivered straight to the door by express mail. Or straight to the stigma, to use the correct botanical term for the female part of the flower.

And who are the couriers? Many different varieties of bee. Studies show that bees can increase the coffee yield by up to 50 per cent.

In areas where the honeybee has not been introduced, more than 30 different species of solitary bees work amid the coffee flowers. Solitary bees are species where every female takes sole responsibility for her own children – unlike social bees, where most individuals are sterile but help bring up the queen's offspring.

Social bees like honeybees are also good at pollinating coffee, so coffee producers used to be encouraged to keep colonies of these bees near their coffee plantations. However, the prevailing view nowadays is that introducing honey bees may displace diverse solitary bees, who do a better job overall.

In order for solitary bees to thrive, it is important for there to be enough nesting places for them near the coffee plantation. Some species need small patches of bare earth for their nest, while others live in hollows in old or dead trees. The traditional method of cultivating coffee – in small fields of coffee bushes surrounded by woodland – is a far better way of ensuring pollination than a plantation in full sunlight. What's more, shade-grown coffee tastes better.

And while we're on the subject of flavour, did you know that the world's ultimate luxury coffee is really crappy, in the literal sense of the word? When a coffee bean passes through an animal's intestines, some of the components are broken down and the coffee bean that emerges is sweeter and less bitter.

This remarkable discovery started with the Asian palm civet, a member of the viverrid family. It lives in the tropical rainforests of Indonesia, where it enjoys a varied diet of small animals and fruit, including familiar exotics such as mango, rambutan and – yes, that's right – the beans of the coffee plant. Don't ask me who, but somebody struck on the idea of extracting semi-digested coffee beans from the dung of the Asian palm civet and selling them for a stiff price. We're talking about almost £50 for a cup of civet coffee!

This started off as a nice sideline for small-scale Indonesian farmers, who began to collect wild civet dung. But once people realised there was good money to be made, they started capturing and caging the civets, which were then force-fed coffee beans under miserable conditions. An absolutely wretched business, to be avoided at all costs.

If you must insist on mucking around with £50 cups of coffee, why not go for the elephant-dung variant instead?

It's produced by the Golden Triangle Asian Elephant Foundation, a charitable foundation dedicated to the protection of elephants. Three days after a coffee bean enters at the trunk end, it is picked out of the dung at the tail end, which apparently gives the coffee a raisin-like flavour.

Personally, I'd rather stick to straightforward shade-grown coffee with some raisins on the side!

Redder Strawberries and Better Tomatoes, Thanks to Insects

We have gradually come to realise that insect pollination is crucial for increasing the yield of crops of different fruits and berries, but did you know that insect pollination also helps to improve the quality of the berries?

Take strawberries, for example, which are not berries in strictly botanical terms but so-called false fruit – a swollen, juicy flower base covered in fruits (or actually nuts, botanically speaking, just to complicate matters further). The point is that each of the small pale 'seeds' on the outside of a strawberry is actually a tiny fruit, and as many of these as possible must develop in order for the strawberry to become big and juicy. If only a few of these 'seeds' develop, the strawberry will be small and knobbly. A well-pollinated strawberry may have 400–500 'seeds' and it takes insects to make that happen.

A German study shows that insect-pollinated straw-berries are redder, firmer and less ill-shapen than those that are wind- or self-pollinated. Firmer berries may not only be tastier, but also cope better with transport and storage, meaning they last longer in the shops, and this in turn means the strawberry farmers are better paid for the berries they have grown. The market value of insect-pollinated strawberries was 39 per cent higher than that of wind-pollinated strawberries and as much as 54 per cent higher than that of self-pollinated strawberries.

Similar effects are seen in numerous other insect-pollinated food plants. Apples become sweeter, blue-berries bigger, rape seeds have higher oil content, while melons and cucumbers are firmer fleshed. Even where gardeners have run around the tomato greenhouse with a vibrating wand that imitates the quiver of a bumblebee shaking loose the pollen the taste panel is merciless in its judgement: insect-pollinated tomatoes simply taste better.

Food for Our Food

Producing honey and ensuring pollination are not the only useful services insects perform for us and our food, they also form a vital part of the staple diet of the animals many humans like to eat, including larger species such as fish and birds.

Freshwater fish live largely off insects. Because some insects take infant swimming so seriously that they keep their young permanently submerged until they reach the age of reason: mosquitoes, mayflies and dragonflies, to name but a few. Many of the insect babies end up as snacks for trout and perch down there. And then we humans eat the fish. So, you can thank the insects next time you sit down to a trout supper.

Birds are also eager insect-eaters. More than 60 per cent of the world's bird species are insect eaters. Insects are particularly important as food for the chicks of some species, who are in serious need of protein-rich food to grow big and strong. Some of the birds us humans like hunting and eating, such as pheasants, grouse and ptarmigans, are dependent on juicy insect larvae as chicks.

We humans can use insects as a source of nourishment too. The UN estimates that more than a quarter of the world's population consumes insects as part of its diet. Insects are most commonly eaten in Asian, African and South American countries, but our European culture also has a certain tradition of this. The Bible provides a precise description of which insects may be eaten – although the understanding of species isn't quite up to modern-day standards (insects have six legs, not four):

All flying insects that creep on all fours shall be an abom-
ination to you. Yet these you may eat of every flying insect
that creeps on all fours: those which have jointed legs
above their feet with which to leap on the Earth.

Leviticus 11: 20–21,

New King James Version

This is often interpreted as meaning that orthopterans are
fine, while other insects are unclean. And we know that
locusts were considered a delicacy in ancient times: stone
reliefs from around 700 BCE show skewered locusts being
brought out for the king.

Insects Are Healthy,
Environmentally Friendly Food

Insects are actually a very nutritious food. Of course, it
depends on the type of insect, but generally speaking, they
have the protein content of beef with very little of the fat.
They also have many other important nutrients: cricket
flour may contain more calcium than milk and twice as
much iron as spinach. And it's not just healthy to eat insects,
it may be environmentally smart too. Replacing some of our
current livestock with mini-livestock such as grasshoppers
or mealworm beetles could help make food production considerably more sustainable. For some people, it could also

ease the transition to a diet based less on meat and more on plants.

Because, as we know, we're pressed for space on this planet. There are already more than seven billion of us humans here and 140 newcomers are added every minute. This is equivalent to a net monthly increase the size of the population of Scotland. And when it comes to putting food in all these mouths, insects are a much more efficient option than our traditional domestically farmed animals. It is estimated that, at their best, grasshoppers are 12 times more efficient than cattle at converting fodder to protein.

What's more, they consume only a fraction of the water a cow does, and produce almost no dung – unlike cows, which really crap on the environment, so to speak. They produce tonnes and tonnes of dung every year, and emit a hefty dose of methane and other climate gases on top of that. There's very little of that kind of muck in insect dung.

To cut a long story short: insect mini-livestock requires very little space, food and water, reproduces at a tremendous rate, and simultaneously provides an effective source of nutrient-rich food that is high in protein and emits minimal amounts of climate gas.

Could it get any better? Well, yes, actually it could. Because insects can also be raised on our food waste (*see page 130*). This means we can kill two birds (or grasshoppers) with one stone, producing good food and eliminating our waste problem at the same time. More research is needed into this area if we seriously intend to include insects in our diet or the diet of our livestock, and this is certainly a growing area of interest. One of the promising initiatives is to farm black soldier fly larvae on food waste. These maggot-like critters are capable of transforming four times their own bodyweight per day into both feed and compost. Harvested in their last larval stage or as a pupae, when their nutritional value peaks, they can be used as feed for fish, poultry, pigs and even dogs. They are also edible for humans and can have a protein content as high as 40 per cent. In addition, the leftover frass (leftover feed, exoskeletons and droppings) from production can be used as fertiliser for plants. As almost one-third of all food produced for human consumption is lost or wasted every year, according to The Food and Agriculture Organization of the United Nations (FAO), so the potential for alternative solutions here is certainly enormous.

Bug Grub

If using insects for human consumption is to yield any environmental benefits, it won't be a matter of scattering a few fried ants on our salad, or decorating confectionery with chocolate-coated grasshoppers. Those stunts where people serve up whole insects are mostly just for novelty's sake.

Just as we don't eat lamb steak with the wool on, insects will also need to be processed to transform them into tempting foodstuffs. And we must produce them in quantities that make the finished product cheap and easily available. Only then can cricket-flour protein cakes and mealworm burgers become daily fare.

The term 'Meat-free Monday' has already caught on. Maybe 'Insect Tuesday' will be next?

It may be some time before we start thinking of insects as everyday food in Europe. But how about developing insect-based fodder for livestock or fish in the meantime, using insects that have eaten their way through our organic waste en route to adulthood? That way we could feed our farmed salmon insects instead of soya from Brazil. Research on such topics is happily already underway.

Using insects as food for humans involves some challenges. Insects have their share of parasites and diseases, which we will have to control if we are to engage in large-scale production. Some people have allergic reactions to insects, and legislation dealing with insects for consumption will need upgrading.

Crucially, we must be certain that this is genuinely sustainable, from a lifecycle perspective too – that heating the mini cattle sheds doesn't eat up all the benefits, for example. Because grasshoppers aren't like hardy sheep breeds that can be kept outside all year: they won't necessarily be able to withstand the climate throughout the year without heating, especially in northern climes. Proper heat levels are crucial to rapid growth and high reproduction.

One major challenge remains: consumer acceptance. Consumers must want to buy and eat insect products because they see them as interesting and relevant food. Perhaps this will come about naturally if cheap and tasty insect flour becomes readily available in the shops. Because we can do this if we want to. It only took us a few years to learn to eat raw fish, after all.

Could insects be the new sushi?

It is also important to find the right way to market these new titbits. Grasshoppers and crickets, which people already eat in so many parts of the world, could, with a little imagination, be repackaged as the land's answer to sea prawns. And we have to use language that sparks positive associations.

Pioneering promoters of the insect diet are on the case. And in the English-speaking world at least, humour seems to be the answer.

Grub Kitchen, a restaurant in Wales, uses punning language to help make the food more palatable – from its name to the often-alliterative offerings on the menu: mealworm macchiato, bug burgers, cricket cookies. Chef Andrew

Holcroft has also pointed out that the language used about the dishes must appeal to the senses: 'Crispy and crunchy descriptions of insects, such as stir-fried or sautéed, sound more appetising than soft-boiled or poached ... [which sound] squelchy and squishy.' In Norway, the word *mushi* has been suggested to promote the softer insect dishes, both to draw on the positive associations of sushi and because it means 'insect' in Japanese.

If You Can't Beat 'Em, Eat 'Em

The nineteenth-century British entomologist Vincent M. Holt was extremely interested in nutrition, especially among Britons of limited means. He thought the working classes should turn to insects as a rich source of nourishment. As early as 1885, the same year in which the Statue of Liberty arrived in New York and Ibsen's *Wild Geese* had its world premiere in Bergen, Holt wrote a neat little pamphlet entitled 'Why Not Eat Insects?' For the occasion, slugs and snails (which are molluscs) and woodlice (crustaceans) were incorporated in the insect world.

Holt argued forcefully that insects would be a healthy and useful addition to the menu. He thought they would spice up the wretched diet that the working classes and manual labourers ate in those days. The peasant should eat the pests in his field for dinner and the woodman should lunch on the fat larvae in the trees he chopped, he suggested. A win-win situation, in other words.

Holt's funny little book also includes plenty of recipes. Unfortunately, perhaps, neither his slug soup nor his fried flounder with woodlouse sauce quite caught on. Perhaps a better choice of raw materials and modern methods of preparation might help combat the lack of enthusiasm for eating insects. Nowadays, the matter is under serious discussion at the UN as well as other forums.

Perhaps the future will prove Holt right in the end: 'While I am confident that they will never condescend to eat us, I am equally confident that, on finding out how good they are, we shall some day right gladly cook and eat them.'

CHAPTER 6

The Circle of Life – and Death:
Insects as Caretakers

I know of few things as beautiful as mighty ancient oaks. There they stand proudly, a legacy from a bygone age; oaks that sprouted and grew before the days of streetlamps and social media, in a time when trolls still lived among the ancient trees and not in the shimmering blue websites on your computer screen.

Today's great oaks have retained their magic. And where Pippi Longstocking once found lemonade, we scientists can go in search of rare insects. Because inside the ancient oak trees, hollows form where the wood slowly rots. Here, it is dim but not quite dark. There is a scent of fungus and damp earth, like a faint suggestion of autumn. At the same time, a sweetish hint of warm timber is like a promise of spring to come. Inside here, you discover another world, a world where the meaning of time and space is altered.

Time goes faster because a beetle lives out its entire life over a single summer. And a fistful of reddish-brown wood mould, with its raw tang of fungus, damp and life's decay, is an entire world for a millimetre-long pseudoscorpion.

Inside here live brightly coloured red velvet mites and pallid beetle babies, enormous scarabs and tiny little springtails. Nurseries and pick-up joints stand side by side. There is life and death, drama and dreams, all on a millimetric scale.

The quest to find ancient oaks and their inhabitants has led me to many forest areas I would never otherwise have seen, and given me many encounters with nature that I wouldn't have missed for the world: picnic spots on the bare, rocky hills of Vestfold, blue mountains in the distance and the warm spring sun upon my face; late spring evenings in Telemark on my way back to the car after the day's work is done, with only the cry of the tawny owl and a sickle moon for company; steep, slippery slopes in Agder that I barely managed to scale in bucketing rain; boulder scree in Western Norway, where all the oaks bear traces of pruning from earlier times when people harvested leaves as winter fodder for their livestock; avenues, pastures, wooded hillocks in cultivated fields, private gardens. Usually solitary – yet never alone. Because more individuals may live in these ancient oak trees than there are human inhabitants in Oslo.

An ancient hollow oak tree is like a fortress. A fortress of biodiversity, no less. The shell of resilient oak wood provides shelter from rain, sun and peckish little birds for the many hundreds of different insect species that live inside the hollow. Reminiscent of the ornamental carvings of intertwining dragons and serpents on stave churches, the intricate oak bark provides a habitat for minuscule pin lichens. Some fungi live in close cohabitation with the roots of the oak, while others help the insects to break down the dead timber.

The factor largely responsible for the presence of all these species is wood mould – a life-giving blend of rotting wood residue, fungal threads, maybe an old bird's nest, and a smidgeon of bat guano. For insects, wood mould is like a gourmet restaurant: even the most exacting bugs will find a menu to suit their tastes here. Hundreds of different critters may live in the dim, humid atmosphere inside a hollow oak, contributing to nature's eternal circle by slowly, slowly converting mighty trees into mould and soil where new acorns can sprout.

Somebody Has to Do the Cleaning

Herbivores consume just one tenth of all the plants that sprout and grow. The remainder, 90 per cent of all plant production, is left lying on the ground. And plants and trees aren't the only things to die; life also comes to an end for animals of all sizes, from midges to moose. As a result, there are impressive amounts of protein and carbohydrate to be recycled. On top of that we have to consider all the waste these creatures produce over their lifetimes – dung, plain and simple, needs to be taken care of too. A pretty crappy job, you might think, but insects are on hand to help us out, as usual.

This is where nature's caretaking service comes in. Just like in schools, offices or blocks of flats, it's often down to the caretaker to clear up after everybody else. And this is how it works in the forests, meadows and our cities, too, where thousands of fungi and insects perform the thoroughly crucial task of decomposing dead organic matter. Nature's tiny caretakers devour all the mess on the spot. It can take time and it requires sophisticated collaboration in which different species have different roles to play.

And even though very few of us think about it as we are taking our Sunday stroll through the park or in the forest, these processes of decomposition are crucial to life on Earth. Insects' patient chomping on dried-up trees and rotten remains don't just clear the ground of dung, and dead plants and animals; just as importantly, the insects' contribution returns the nutrients in the dead organic matter to the soil. Indeed, if substances like nitrogen and carbon are not returned to the earth, it will be impossible for new life to grow.

Dead Trees as Beetle Abodes

When the insect mum is house hunting in the forest, her priorities are different from those of us humans. Take beetles that live in dead trees, for example: whereas we fear damp damage and rot, beetles think they're fantastic because they're like a fridgeful of food for the family's greedy kids.

So, Madame Beetle goes for a viewing. Softly, she sets down all six legs on the dead tree. With antennae and toes, she tastes and smells the spot where she's landed to see if it will make a good nursery for her beetle babies. If she's satisfied, she swiftly lays her eggs in a little crack in the bark and moves on, in search of more trees in need of care-taking services.

The egg hatches a wee larva that boldly sets about chewing its way through bark and wood – a gargantuan task in which, fortunately, it is not alone. Thousands of beetle larvae may be at work in such dead trees, ably assisted by bacteria and fungi.

New dead wood is fantastic fun: there's plenty of sugary sap beneath the bark, and when it ferments there's a real party atmosphere among the visitors. Every type of wood has its beetle specialists, who greedily gorge on this platter. Bark beetles are a typical example. But speed is of the essence because by the end of the first summer the platter is empty: all that lovely sugar is gone.

By contrast, however, dead dry timber is a pretty dismal lunch for a beetle. Cellulose and lignin, two of the most important components of timber, are about as juicy and digestible for an insect as a sack of bran would be for us, so it's a good thing some fungi just adore cellulose and others love lignin. They cast their fungal threads into the wood, making it more appealing to the beetles because the nutritional content increases and becomes more accessible. Bacteria also provide a great garnish. Some beetles even have tiny collaborating partners in their bodies that help them to extract nourishment from even the most indigestible parts of the tree. All in all, myriads of organisms are involved in the decomposition of dead wood.

Dead Wood Lives!

Dead trees, branches and roots are home to a surprisingly large number of species. As many as 6,000 species live in dead wood in the Nordic countries – a third of all the species we find in our forests! In fact, approximately 3,000 of these are insects. By comparison, there are only around 300 bird species and fewer than 100 mammals in the region.

Once fungi and insects, mosses and lichens, and bacteria have moved in, there are more living cells in the dead tree than there were when it was alive. So ironically enough, dead trees are actually among the most living things you can find in the forest. And every species has its particular cleaning job to do, not to mention having its own precise demands when it comes to the kind of dead wood it wants to live in or on.

So why are there so many species in dead wood? Part of the reason is that insects that live on dead timber have differing demands when it comes to the type of dead wood they're after. For us humans, who don't find timber toothsome, it is difficult to grasp all the nuances when it comes to types of wood, stages of decomposition, size and surroundings. But to insects, a dead spruce tree is quite different from a dead birch. And an aspen that has just died is quite unlike an aspen that has lain dead in the forest for several years. As I mentioned earlier (*see page 86*), plants and trees have an active, species-specific defence against grazing animals and insects. This persists after the tree's death, especially early on, meaning that the first insect arrivals at the newly dead tree must be specially adapted to cope with this.

Size is also important: a dead oak branch offers a totally different habitat to the rotted innards of a giant oak. And a dead resinous pine tree on a hill in the baking sunlight is home to totally different species with different dietary habits than a dead pine in a dark, dense forest. In other words, a stick isn't just a stick: dead timber has more nuances than a fine wine and many insects are exacting connoisseurs. Since insects have such differing demands, there need to be enough of all these various types of dead wood in the forest to provide sufficient housing to enable every insect to find its own little hovel and get its job done.

But there's one more vital point when the beetle mum is hunting for a likely dead tree trunk in which to house her children. The window of opportunity is short in the insect housing market and it's a question of getting to the suitable tree in time. If the distance between rare and specific types of log (like large-diameter oak trunks) is too large, as is often the case in modern managed forest, the beetles dependent on such logs might not be able to get there at all.

That is why natural forest is so important: forest that isn't affected by modern logging. It contains much more dead timber than managed forests, and there is a great deal more variety in the dead wood, which means there are more beetle homes on the market. They are so close together that the beetle mum can pop into several of them in a single evening of viewings, laying a few eggs here and there. That's the way to create beetle diversity.

Cracking Research

The goings-on in dead trees are among my absolute favourite topics, and a subject we do a lot of research into in the research group I belong to. It may not all be 'rocket science', but we've certainly been involved in some projects that went with a bang. Like 15 years ago, when we did a really cracking experiment: we wound metres of detonating cord around trees in the forest, 5 metres above the ground, and lit the fuse. And then we ran ... With an enormous bang the trunk was blown right off and the top of the tree crashed to earth!

The point of this exercise was to create standing dead trees. We created 60 such trees and in each of the years that followed we checked which beetles were visiting the dead trees. This taught us a great deal about different insects' dietary preferences. We also saw that the forestry sector's environmental measures of tree retention – leaving trees in the clearcuts that eventually become high stumps – actually work.

What's even more fun is that now, some 15 years later, we can hear a kind of echo from those earlier beetle visits.

It turns out that these days there are different fungi on the trees depending on which insects paid a visit all those years ago! That made us wonder whether fungi and beetles have become a bit like bees and flowers – are they mutually useful? Perhaps certain wood fungi simply hitch a ride with certain beetles and get dropped off at the restaurant door? We know of some bark beetles where the collaboration is so close that both parties depend upon it. But could this collaboration be much more common than that in a looser form – without co-dependency but with advantages for both parties?

To check this out, one of our PhD students has been putting trees in cages – or rather parts of trees, strictly speaking. She cut down living trees, made logs of identical sizes from them and randomly chose which logs to cage. Logs that were caged did not receive insect visits, as the bugs couldn't get through the netting of the cage. For the purposes of comparison, the other logs were placed outside the cages, so that insects could land as usual.

It turned out that the fungal society was totally different in the logs that insects couldn't access. We think this is because many insects carry spores or fungal 'threads', either on their body or in their guts. When the insect lands on a newly dead log to lay eggs, this fungus is sprinkled or excreted along with the insect dung, and thereby finds a new home.

In addition – and this is the really exciting bit – our study showed that the caged logs decomposed more slowly. Quite simply, the cleaning job takes longer when the insects don't get to help.

A Kindergarten Beneath Your Shoes

I love running, especially on soft forest paths. A half-hour run from my home takes me to a forest reserve strewn with dead trees, like a game of pick-up sticks. I can look around and try to count species, of which there are around 20,000 in Norwegian forests. Of course, not all of them live in 'my' forest, but still – how many can I see? I can count several trees, a dozen plants, lichen, fungi, perhaps an elk or a large bird if I move quietly. If it's summer, the insects will do wonders for my list of species, but even so, I barely spot more than a hundred, even here in the reserve. So where are all the other tens of thousands of species?

An awful lot of the other species are tiny insects and related creatures that live out their lives in hiding. As mentioned, a third of forest species live in and on dead trees. The other important habitat is the soil, because there is no other place where species are packed together so densely. The tiny patch of earth stuck to the sole of my running shoes after a trip to the forest may be home to more bacteria than there are human beings in the US, not to mention thousands of thin fungal threads. Here in the soil, you also find a myriad of important critters and small insects. A whole zoo of little creatures lives down there in the darkness: earthworms and mites, roundworms, pot worms, springtails, and woodlice. All these species – that we don't give a hoot about on a day-to-day basis – have important jobs in the recycling sector: they chew and dig and air and mix. In the blink of an eye, rubbish has been reconverted into soil, ready to sprout new life. It's pretty miraculous, really.

Soil is important, but masses of it vanishes every year. Not because runners dash off with chunks of it stuck to their trainers but because of erosion: erosion by wind and water. Some of this is natural but in many places the soil loss is high because we humans have removed natural vegetation. Consequently, there's nothing left to retain the soil, which is blown away or runs off into the sea, and elsewhere. This is losing us billions of tonnes of topsoil every year – and along with the soil, we are losing crucial diversity of decomposers, which are our guarantee that the recycling of nutrients will continue.

The thin layer of earth is the planet's skin: a thin, living layer over the magma (the layer of molten or semi-molten rock) and the rocky crust. Perhaps we ought to pay a little more attention to the Earth's skincare? Like a teenager anxiously checking his or her complexion in the mirror, we, too, should be aware of the wellbeing of the topsoil and forest soil, along with all their inhabitants. Because we need them and – to stick to the language of the cosmetics industry – because they're worth it.

An Ant in Manhattan

Finger food at festivals, picnics in the park ... The summer propels us and our meals out into the city. But what about the scraps of food – the bits of hamburger we drop on the pavement, or the hotdog bun left lying on the lawn? This is where ants come into the picture.

Many people think of ants as a nuisance, even yucky, but it's actually good to have them around, in the urban environment too. A group of insect scientists studying ants in Manhattan did a back-of-the-envelope calculation and estimated that there are 2,000 ants for every person in the city. And what do ants do there? They live out their tiny lives, which mostly consist of food gathering and reproduction. When it comes to diet they are undemanding and have a healthy appetite too. Another of the scientists' back-of-the-envelope calculations estimates that the scraps of junk food put away by the ants of Manhattan add up to the equivalent of 60,000 hotdogs a year! It's a damn good thing we have them.

In an experiment, scientists compared how much food

waste found its way into ant bellies in different parts of Manhattan. Precisely weighed quantities of food were set out in tiny little 'food scrap cafés' in parks and central reservations. The scientists offered the ants a comprehensive fast-food package, New York style: hotdogs, crisps and a cookie for dessert. At the same time, they measured the species richness of ants and other small, urban bugs in the same places, establishing that there were more species of ants (and other bugs) in the parks than in the central reservations of a busy street.

Because it has been shown that food gathering in many other natural systems is more efficient in a species-rich society, the scientists expected the park ants to eat more of the food scraps than the central reservation ants, but the result they got in Manhattan was the polar opposite: the central reservation ants carried off more than twice as many scraps. There may be several reasons for this. First off, it is warmer on the central reservations. And since ants are cold-blooded creatures, everything goes faster when the temperature is high.

Secondly, it seems that a European immigrant, the pavement ant, really has a taste for American junk food. This species was much more common in the central reservations than in the parks, and wherever it was present, up to three times more fast food scraps vanished than when it wasn't. In other words, environmental conditions and individual species turned out to be more important than species diversity when it came to cleaning up Manhattan's food scraps.

Pavement ants are territorial and, like other urban gangs, they fiercely defend their little patch of the city against interlopers. But the ant gang isn't alone on the streets of Manhattan: there are regular rounds of gang violence with rats, which are less common but bigger. They want their share of the junk food plunder. These clashes between gangs ought to be of some interest to us humans, who are even bigger, because although mice and rats make a positive contribution in the sense that they eat our food scraps, they are also notorious transmitters of disease. The same can hardly be said of ants. This means ants are much better suited to the task of clean-up patrol in the city's outdoor spaces.

It is time to acknowledge that even our cities are ecological systems in which crawling critters are an essential ingredient. On the central reservation on Broadway alone there are 13 different ant species. In all, 40 ant species have been found in New York – that's almost two-thirds of the ant species in the UK as a whole. And since more than half of the world's (human) population now lives in cities, we ought to spend more time finding out how urban ecosystems operate.

The thing is, urban nature also performs significant

services for the ecosystem. Trees provide shade, muffle noise, and clean the air. Green areas absorb water after heavy rainfall and reduce flooding. Open water cools, and the species in ponds and streams filter the water, making it cleaner. The tiniest patch of earth can provide a habitat for masses of useful bugs that pollinate plants, spread seeds or clean up the streets – like ants.

Economists in Oslo have also studied the city's ecosystem services and their worth. An attempt to quantify the value of the green structures in and around the capital to the health and wellbeing of the inhabitants – by calculating their time-use value, among other measures – added up to millions of pounds.

And that was without including the value of the ants' contribution.

Greater knowledge of urban ecology will enable us to plan and maintain our cities better. Even something as simple as raking the central reservations less frequently has proven important, as it ensures more hiding places and a happier life – if you happen to be an adventurous Manhattan ant!

A Troublesome Fly

Hotdogs on the streets of big cities are one thing, but there are also other types of dead meat that need to be cleared away out in the natural world. Think of all the animals, big and small, that die and are left lying where they dropped. It would be quite unpleasant if they didn't get recycled pretty sharpish.

From the insects' point of view, carcasses are a rather handy source of food – they can't run away and they can't defend themselves. But the insects have to be quick because carcasses are rich in nutrients and therefore much sought-after food; what's more, the competition includes a large range of species of varying sizes. Here, insects are literally in the flyweight class, whereas their opponents are heavyweights such as foxes and ravens, vultures and hyenas. One trick is to lay not eggs but ready-hatched larvae in the carcass, as some flesh flies from the *Sarcophaga* family do. Another is to eat quickly, grow even more quickly and generally be flexible when it comes to how big you need to be before pupating.

Another cunning solution is to hide the carcass by burying it. The beautiful red-and-black sexton beetles of the *Nicrophorus* family are masters of such vanishing acts. They work in pairs, digging out soil from underneath the carcass and placing earth on top, and in this way can totally wipe a dead mouse off the face of the Earth in a single day. Beneath the earth, they wrap the carcass up in a ball and lay their eggs. And despite the slightly jaw-dropping choice of nursery, they are attentive parents. They chew off tiny scraps of carcass and regurgitate them into the mouths of their larvae, which are incapable of digesting the food themselves to begin with. This is one of the few examples of parental care in the insect world other than among the social insects (*see page 55*).

Sexton beetles also have some good friends that are not insects. When the newly hatched sexton beetles leave their childhood home, masses of tiny mites climb onto them and hitch a ride to the next carcass. This species of mite only lives with sexton beetles: it cannot fly and is reliant on transport to find its way to a new, fresh carcass. In return for the lift, the mites eat up the eggs and larvae of other competing fly species in the carcass.

The decomposing crew that turns up to break down the carcass belongs to a segment of the insect world that is rarely mentioned or rewarded. There are no fan groups for sexton beetles as there are for bumblebees, yet they are tremendously important creatures.

In South Asia, people have learnt to their cost what can happen when carrion eaters vanish. It's true that the creature in question was the vulture, who might be said to be the blow fly's massively big brother, and enjoys a similarly bad reputation among most people. Nonetheless, the point is the same. Around the turn of the millennium, the veterinary medication diclofenac was introduced into India as a treatment for sick cows. Just 15 years later, the medicine had dispatched an insane 99 per cent of all the country's vultures because residual amounts of the substance were left in dead cows and were passed onto the vultures that ate them. The vultures suffered kidney failure and died. Although scavenging insects almost certainly worked at top gear, they were unable to deal with such large amounts of carrion alone. As a result, dead cows were left lying on the ground. Once the vultures had vanished, other large scavengers appeared on the scene – feral dogs, whose numbers exploded. Since many of them are rabies carriers, the population boom in dogs that resulted from the disappearance of the natural carrion eater has been blamed for an additional 48,000 rabies deaths in the Indian population.

Carrion eaters can also help the police in their criminal investigations because there is a pattern to when which species come to a corpse, and this can be used to help connect the dots in criminal investigations, and ultimately solve crimes. The first time insects helped identify a murderer is said to have occurred in a little Chinese village in 1235. A man was brutally murdered with a sickle and the local peasants were called into a meeting. They were instructed to bring their sickles with them. The investigator made them wait and, since it was a hot, sunny day, it wasn't long before flies appeared. When all the flies landed on the same sickle, the owner was so shocked that he confessed on the spot. With their peerless sense of smell, the flies were drawn to the traces of blood even though the sickle had been cleaned.

Today, the methods are more advanced but the basic principles remain the same: insect species appear in a dead body in a given order and following a particular logic. This fact can be used to calculate the time of death and may, in some cases, also tell you something about the cause of death. Drugs and toxins accumulate in the insects present and thus they can be more easily detected. Such chemical substances also affect the growth rate of feeding maggots, and therefore provide important information when forensic entomologists are estimating the time passed since death occurred.

Moreover, species are distributed over defined geographies. Knowledge of this can be used to determine whether a body has been moved if the species that are present are normally widespread in quite different areas or in other parts of the country. One example of this was a case where a body was found in a sugar-cane field in Hawaii. The oldest larvae found in the corpse belonged to a fly that lives primarily in urban areas. Indeed, it turned out that the corpse had been kept in a flat in Honolulu for a couple of days before being dumped in the field.

Insects can also make a more indirect contribution to crime solving. In the US, insects mashed into a car's radiator grille were used to trap a killer. He claimed to have been on the East Coast when his family was murdered in California, but the species found on his hire car could only be found on the West Coast.

When Nature Calls and Insects Answer

All animals eliminate waste in the form of dung. Dung from large creatures, like mammals, represents a significant biomass. It may still contain useful nutrients but it also has large quantities of bacteria, disease-causing parasites and things the body wants to expel. Not all creatures are up to eating this but insects stand ready. Beetles and flies are particularly likely to have muck on their menu. Certain expertise is required in this working group: a good sense of smell and rapid reflexes. When the battle for cowpats is under way, you have to be quick if you want to secure your slice of the pie.

Some participants, like the horn fly, are renowned for starting to lay their eggs before the cowpat is even finished. This is dangerous, but some parents will go to any lengths to ensure the best conditions for their kids to grow up in. Because fresh dung goes quickly, especially when warm, you might say it sells like hot cakes. For example, one study showed that as many as 4,000 dung beetles fell upon a 5-decilitre dollop of elephant dung doled out by researchers in a mere 15 minutes. Other studies found that it took a couple of hours for 1.5 kilos of elephant dung to virtually vanish off the face of the Earth once 16,000 dung beetles had gone in and done their job.

Dung beetles have three main strategies: dweller, tunneller or roller.

The dweller variant likes to live right in the middle of the meal. It crawls down into the dung, content to eat and lay its eggs there. Many Norwegian dung beetles (members of the *Aphodiinae* subfamily) belong to this category. The dweller strategy is risky – you never know how many others are laying their eggs in the same dung and in the worst-case scenario the larvae may eat each other out of house and home, and all end up starving to death.

One way of avoiding this is to build an extension for the kids, with its own pantry. This is the technique used by the tunnellers. They dig passages beneath or right beside the dung; tunnels that can range in length from a decimetre to a metre. We often find the longest passageways in species where the dung beetle mother and father work together – they drag small balls or rolls of muck down into the end of their tunnel, and it then serves as a kids' room for the larvae.

The most advanced variant are the rollers, who grab their share of food and make a swift exit. They pack the dung into a ball, which can often weigh 50 times more than the beetle itself, and trundle off – always in a straight line, regardless of whether the sun is hidden behind a cloud or it's a dark, starry night. So, how do they do it?

Creative scientists have really gone to town on their field experiments: Some placed tiny peaked caps on the beetles' heads to shade them from the sun. Others used large mirrors to manipulate the position of the sun or moon. The most creative of all was, perhaps, the researcher who moved the entire experiment into the Johannesburg Planetarium and proved that dung beetles can use the Milky Way to orientate themselves! The only other creatures known to use the stars for orientation are human beings, seals and some birds. All in all, the research shows that the dung-rollers can steer their course using the positions of both sun and moon, as well as polarised light or the Milky Way.

These particular beetles have fascinated humans for thousands of years. The dung-rolling *Scarabaeus sacer* plays a central role in Egyptian mythology. When the Egyptians saw these beetles trundling off with round balls of dung it reminded them of the sun's journey across the heavens. The beetle became their 'sacred scarab', symbolising Khepri, god of the rising sun. This insect god is sometimes portrayed as a beetle and sometimes as a person with a beetle's head.

The Egyptians also saw how the scarab beetles were among the first living things to emerge on the muddy banks of the Nile after the spring floods. Where the old dung beetles had buried their balls of dung, new young beetles clambered up out of the earth a few weeks later. From here, it wasn't much of a leap to make a link between the sacred scarab, and renewal and reincarnation. It became common for scarab amulets to be used by the living and to be bound into the bandages that swathed mummies.

Perhaps the Egyptians even got the idea of mummification from the beetles, because what does a beetle pupa look like, if not a mummy? It has even been suggested – somewhat playfully, perhaps – that the pyramids are sacred representations of piles of dung, in which the dead pharaoh lies like a mummified pupa, waiting for the metamorphosis of reincarnation.

Dung Does So Much

Dung can be used for so many things. In many cultures, dried cowpats, for example, are still used as fuel or building material. In the insect world, too, we see examples of creative use of excrement. How about a dung wig, for example? The *Hemisphaerota cyanea* leaf beetle lives in dwarf palms in Florida and the neighbouring states. As the larva chews its way through a palm leaf, beautiful pale yellow curly locks ooze out at the opposite end. The larva arranges these pale threads of dung neatly over its back until it ends up with a whole wig. The point of the wig is, of course, self-defence: no matter how hungry you are, you're unlikely to fancy a mouthful of hair.

Several leaf beetle larvae adopt similar techniques but instead of using hair, they count on intimidating and scaring off the enemy. The pale green *Cassida viridis* is common in Europe. Its larvae fashion a kind of roof or parasol out of old larva skin and black lumps of dung that they hold over themselves with the aid of a special 'anal fork'. If an enemy comes too close, the larva can brandish its dung parasol, which may also contain poisonous substances that the larva has produced from the leaves it eats in order to keep enemies at bay.

Case-bearing leaf beetles (from the *Cryptocephalinae* family) are even more advanced. Their children are equipped with something akin to a mobile home made of poo: the mother lays every egg in a beautifully formed container that she moulds from her own excrement. When the egg hatches, the larva opens the door and sticks out its head and legs so that it can carry its house wherever it goes. As the larva itself defecates, it adds to its mobile home, thereby ensuring that it is always big enough. When it's time to pupate, the larva climbs inside and shuts the door behind it. There it can lie, nice and safe, until it has become an adult beetle – and the whole process starts all over again.

A Whole Ecosystem in a Pelt

Some people think sloths are cute. You know, *sloths* – the ones who were portrayed as the incredibly slow but smiley clerks in Disney's *Zootopia*. I actually got up close to a sloth one time in the wild – and I didn't find it in the slightest bit sweet!

I was sitting on the outskirts of a village in Nicaragua with my back to a fallow area – half-open forestland with bare earth. It was pouring with rain. I heard a noise behind me and turned towards the forest. And there, just a few metres away – slowly, slowly, gaze fixed firmly on me – came the most peculiar creature I had ever seen, slinking towards me, sopping wet. This was 30 years ago now, but I clearly remember thinking: *Good God, it looks like a nuclear mutant!*

One biology degree and many years later, I realised this must have been a rare sight. Sloths are one of very few genuinely tree-living mammals and spend the absolute minimum of time on the ground. But once a week the time comes for them to do their business and, oddly enough, they have to do it on the ground. That's when they tend to die, because they are so incredibly slow and can barely defend themselves.

The last thing that occurred to me was to count the toes on the forepaws of this slightly terrifying creature with its fixed grin. Now I know that there are two groups of sloths, three-toed and two-toed, and a few different species within each group. The two- and three-toed variants are very different – it's the three-toed kind we'll be dealing with here.

Neither did it occur to me to go over to the animal and search for butterflies in its brownish-green pelt. I regret that now because sloths carry an entire ecosystem in their fur – a fact we have only recently grasped. Because why should three-toed sloths risk going to the loo on the ground instead of just letting rip from the treetops instead? Especially considering that they expend 8 per cent of their daily calorie intake on these climbing trips and risk getting eaten to boot. Scientists have long sought an explanation. Could the point be to provide manure for the tree they are living in, or were they communicating with other sloths via their latrines?

That wasn't it. In the pelt of the three-toed sloth lives a creature entertainingly known as a sloth moth. When the sloth goes for a toilet break, the moth climbs out of its pelt and lays some eggs in the poo. The larva lives there happily and when it grows into an adult moth, all it has to do is wait for the sloth's next comfort break to be able to move into a safe, warm sloth pelt.

And this is when the fun really starts, because surely the sloth wouldn't bother to risk its life just to do a moth a favour? Well, it turns out that this business involves some advantages for the sloth too.

The moths excrete, die and decompose in the pelt. This increases the nutritional content of the pelt and improves conditions for a type of algae that grows on sloth hair (and absolutely nowhere else in the world, just so you know). The sloth eats this green algae growth by licking it off its fur. The alga has a crucial advantage: it contains important nutrition that the sloth cannot get from its monotonous plant diet. The algae can also serve as camouflage.

So, to sum up: the moth is good for the alga, the alga is good for the sloth, the sloth is good for the moth. It's a whole tiny ecosystem – all in one animal pelt.

Other large animals also play host to dung insects that have found it wisest to stay close to the source rather than spend their entire lives on the lookout for fresh muck. Among kangaroos and our hairy ape brothers, certain beetles simply set up home in the pelt close to the animal's rear end, so there are a few benefits to having a hairless rear that probably hadn't occurred to you.

Drowning in Dung

In 1788, the first cow to set her four hooves on Australian soil arrived. Along with her came a rather motley crew of 1,480 men, women, and children – mostly convicts – along with 87 chickens, 35 ducks, 29 sheep, 18 pheasants and various other things. This marked the end of the Aborigines' 40,000 years of isolation, not to mention the animal and plant life, which had been isolated since the Australian continent split away from Antarctica somewhere between 40 and 85 million years before. Consequently, the continent was full of species that existed nowhere else on the planet – 84 per cent of the mammals and 86 per cent of the plants in Australia were unique.

The four cows and two oxen that accompanied the first European fleet were picked up during the crossing. They came from Cape Town and were zebus, a race of cattle accustomed to a hot climate. One convict called Edward Corbett was given the job of herding the animals, with strict instructions not to let the cattle out of his sight. Alas, just a few months after Daisy had ambled down the gangplank, she and the other cattle vanished – they'd taken off while the herder was having supper.

It was a minor catastrophe: the six cattle were supposed to be used for breeding, milk and food. The settlers could find no familiar edible plants in Australia. Even though they had grain for planting, many of the prisoners had no experience with agriculture and weren't especially keen to learn either. They weren't even any good at fishing. The provisions disappeared fast, despite ultra-strict rationing, so there was great rejoicing when they found the cattle again a few years later – by which time they had become a whole herd. They were getting by swimmingly in Australia's pastureland.

After one or two hundred years, joy turned to desperation. Because what do cows do? They feed, chew, belch and poo, and do all of these things on a massive scale. One cow produces as much as 9 tonnes of dung per year, and that's dry weight. The dung of a single cow covers an area the size of five tennis courts each year. And when cows thrive, there get to be a lot of them – with equivalently large numbers of tennis courts' worth of dung.

By around 1900, there were more than a million head of cattle in Australia – but who was going to clear up after them? This brings me to the point of the story: there were no beetles in Australia that could decompose the cow dung. Or rather there were, of course, some native dung beetles, but they had been reared on dry, hard marsupial dung for millions of years. They certainly had very little taste for foreign cuisine in the form of the zebus's mushy manure. Therefore, the dung was just left lying on the ground, where it dried into a crust that could not be penetrated by so much as a blade of grass. At the height of the problem, up to 2,000 square kilometres of grazing land per year were becoming unusable. In around 1960, roughly 200 years after the arrival of the first cattle, large areas of the country lay fallow because of dung that had not been decomposed.

The only things that could be bothered with the dung were the flies, but they didn't exactly help. In Australia there's a type of fly that resembles the European housefly, except that it lives anywhere *other* than in houses – and now it was particularly keen on living wherever dung happened to be lying around unused. This troublesome fly bred massively, as did other flies that plague humans and livestock – an increased nuisance factor on top of the problem of large areas of fallow land no longer suitable for grazing.

New beetles had to be brought into play. A large-scale project was set in motion, sponsored by the government and the meat industry. Over a period of 15 years, Australian entomologists experimented with numerous species and after careful testing, they set out 1.7 million individuals from 43 different dung beetle species.

The project was a success. More than half of the species became established. The dung disappeared and the plague of flies dwindled notably. Before, only a tiny share (15 per cent) of the nitrogen in the cowpats was being returned to the soil; the beetles' caretaking service increased the level to as much as 75 per cent. This example shows just how important decomposition is for nature and for us humans.

Despite their importance, things aren't looking so good for dung beetles as a group. Globally, 15 per cent of these species are threatened. In Norway, more than half of the roughly 70 types of beetle that live in dung are listed as threatened or near threatened with extinction, and 13 species have apparently already vanished from the country. Norwegian dung beetles are having a particularly tough time in the south – which provides a habitat for species that require fresh cow muck, preferably on sand or unfertilised pastureland beneath a warm summer sun. Changes in agriculture are largely to blame for the disappearance of the dung beetles. Uncultivated pastureland becomes overgrown or is not grazed continuously over time.

Another problem is the widely used parasite treatment Ivermectin, which is given to cattle and other livestock all over the world. The substance has been found to be excreted in the dung in large amounts, and to harm the dung beetles that come to clean up. This may have consequences for both species diversity and speed of decomposition. To reduce the negative effects on dung beetles, some have suggested distributing the drug only by injections to reduce the amount excreted in dung, and only to creatures where parasitic infections are severe. Such restrictions could also help in delaying the increasing resistance in the parasites to Ivermectin.

Our Research into Hollow Oaks

Life in the hollow oaks is in trouble too. The work we have done in my research group shows that the specialised insects that live in hollow oaks are struggling. In many cases, we have found individual species in very few places, perhaps just a couple of oak trees. These special species need areas with many coarse trees that are exposed to the sun – trees that contain a lot of wood mould. There are few such oaks.

Along with other scientists and assistants, I have researched insect life in hollow oaks for more than 10 years. We have determined the species of more than 185,000 different beetle individuals from as many as 1,400 unique species in hollow oaks. Some of these are specialists that live solely in oaks, or solely in hollow trees, preferably oaks. Around 100 beetle species that live in hollow trees are threatened or near threatened with extinction in Norway.

Today, hollow oak trees enjoy special legal status in Norway: they are deemed to be a 'selected habitat type' precisely because they are associated with such rich diversity. These trees' status as a selected habitat type means we must treat them with special care and avoid damaging them. I am involved in a national monitoring programme for hollow oaks, which aims to tell us about their status and development. The hope is to follow this up with a monitoring of the unique insects that live there too.

If we are to secure these fortresses of biodiversity, we must protect the great hollow oaks we still have left. Our research seems to suggest that traces of intensive oak logging several hundred years ago are still reflected in the diversity of beetles in today's hollow oaks. This may be a kind of delayed reaction, known as extinction debt, whereby species cling on for a long time after habitat destruction but are eventually forced to give up the ghost.

We must also make sure that we prevent the areas around oaks that have developed in an open landscape from becoming overgrown. Many of the most specialised insects do best when the sun can shine on the tree, making it snug and warm, and we must take a long-term view, ensuring we recruit new oaks that can become hollow well before the old ones die out.

It takes no time at all to fell a hollow oak standing in the way of progress – a widened road or a new terrace block. Five minutes with a chainsaw and the giant that put out its first shoots in the days of the Black Death, and saw the Renaissance and the Industrial Revolution take shape and pass away, lies splintered on the ground. But it takes 700 years to replace it with a new oak of the same calibre. And where are the insects to live in the meantime?

CHAPTER 7

From Silk to Shellac: Industries of Insects

Throughout history, insects have given us many products of great significance, and many of these products have retained their significance to this day. Some are well known, such as honey and silk. Others you may never have heard of, or even realised that they originated from an insect, like the red colouring in your strawberry jam or the glossy sheen on the skins of supermarket apples.

And, as always in the case of insects, we're talking about enormous numbers. Even the 1.5 billion head of cattle on the planet pale into insignificance when we add up all the livestock in the insect world. According to statistics from the UN's Food and Agriculture Organization, more than 83 billion honeybees buzz around the world in our service. And every year, upwards of 100 billion silkworms sacrifice their lives to provide us with silk.

Wings of Wax

Honeybees make honey, of course, as discussed in Chapter 5 (*see page 104*). But honeybees also make beeswax, a soft mass produced by special glands in their abdomens, which they use to build nurseries, and warehouses for their honey. Beeswax also has many applications for humans and plays a major role in a mythological tale that will be familiar to many.

In Greek mythology, Daedalus and his son Icarus flee Crete using wings that Daedalus has created from birds' feathers and beeswax. Daedalus cautions his son against the dangers of complacency and arrogance before they set off: if Icarus doesn't make enough of an effort, he'll end up flying too low and the sea will destroy his wings. If, on the other hand, he is overcome by hubris and fails to recognise his own limitations, he will fly too high and the sun will melt the beeswax holding his wings together (a psychologist might perhaps note at this point that the father would have been better off telling his son what he *ought* to do instead of teaching him about all the pathways to complete catastrophe). At any rate, young people clearly didn't listen to their parents in those days either: Icarus flew too close to the sun, the wax melted, and he crashed into the ocean. But at least he had a sea (the Icarian Sea, which is part of the Aegean) and an island (Icaria) named after him.

Nowadays, we use beeswax to make candles and cosmetics rather than wings. The Catholic Church has traditionally been a major consumer because the candles used during Mass must be made of beeswax: the pale wax is supposed to symbolise Jesus' body, while the wick at the centre represents his soul. The flame that burns when the wax candle is lit gives us light, while the wax candle itself burns down – sacrificing itself, as Jesus did for humanity. Only the purest wax can be used for this purpose, and bees score high on that count: since nobody had observed them mating, they were long assumed to be virgins who lived a life of sexual abstinence. Only in the 1700s was this misapprehension corrected (*see page 50*), but to this day the rules state that the candles used for Mass in the Catholic Church must contain at least 51 per cent beeswax.

It has become increasingly common to use beeswax in products such as creams and lotions, lip balm and moustache wax. Honey is also an important component of cosmetics, by the way. If, say, you fancy following one of the many recipes for homemade honey facemasks on the Internet, you'll be glad to hear that you are in illustrious company: the wife of the Roman Emperor Nero, Poppaea – who, of course, didn't have the option of ordering products from the online outlets of the finest French cosmetics companies – made her own facemasks from honey mixed with asses' milk. At least that means it doesn't matter if you happen to get some on your lips! Indeed, beeswax mixed with vegetable oils is actually an excellent lip balm.

Beeswax is also used to help oranges, apples and melons keep better, and to make them look shiny and tempting. This familiar foodstuff (E901) is applied to the surface of fruits, nuts and even food supplement pills (as is shellac, *see page 184*). A significant amount of the beeswax extracted from hives these days is also used to produce new beeswax frames that are placed back in the hives – a proper thank-you present!

Silk – a Fabric Fit for a Princess

Silk billows beautifully, is strong but light, cool against the skin, and has a special sheen all of its own. An exclusive fabric, it's hardly surprising that silk from silkworms – the larvae of the *Bombyx mori* butterfly – was long reserved for the Chinese Emperor and those closest to him.

The history of silk reads like a tale from the Arabian Nights: exotic yet brutal, it's difficult to separate fact from fiction. Two strong women play a central role in the legend. In the beginning, 2,600 years before the Western Common Era, the Chinese princess Lei-Tsu sat drinking her tea under a mulberry tree in the garden of the Imperial Palace when a silkworm cocoon fell out of the tree and into the Princess's cup. Lei-Tsu tried to fish it out, but the heat of the liquid dissolved the cocoon, transforming it into the most beautiful thread – long enough to cover the entire garden. And in the very innermost part of the cocoon lay a tiny larva. Lei-Tsu immediately grasped the potential of this discovery and got the Emperor's permission to plant more mulberry trees and breed more silkworms. She taught the women at the Imperial Court to spin the silk into a thread strong enough to be woven, thereby laying the foundations of Chinese silk production.

Silk production would remain an important cultural and economic factor in China for several thousand years. Indeed, the country is still the world's largest silk producer, and to this day, the cocoons are placed in boiling water to kill the larvae and loosen the thin silk threads.

China guarded the secrets of silk for a good long time. Eventually, the trading routes known as the Silk Road opened up between China and the Mediterranean countries, where silk was an important product because the Romans loved it. That said, some viewed this new, almost transparent fabric as immoral; indeed, certain people went so far as to claim that silk dresses were practically an invitation to adultery because they left so little to the imagination.

Be that as it may, we might speculate whether it was actually the amount of gold leaving the Roman Empire to pay for the silk that people found immoral rather than the fabric itself – because China's monopoly on silk production earned the country enormous income. Consequently, people were also strictly forbidden from sharing the secret: attempts to smuggle out silkworm larvae or eggs were punishable by death.

In the end, the secret came out anyway, and once again a woman played a central role, if we are to believe another of the many legends. It is said that a Chinese princess married the Prince of Khotan, a Buddhist kingdom in the west of modern-day China that lay along the Silk Road. On her departure, the princess smuggled out silkworm eggs and mulberry tree seeds in her headdress. In this way, the secret spread, the monopoly was broken and several other countries started to produce silk. Today, more than 200,000 tonnes of silk are produced each year to make clothing, bicycle tyres and surgical thread. Silkworms are still the main producers, although a few other related species are also used.

Hanging By a Thread

Silkworms are not the only insects that spin silk. This skill has probably cropped up more than 20 times among insects over the course of evolution. Green lacewings, for example, fasten their eggs onto small stalks of silk. They resemble tiny Q-tips, with the eggs like a clump at the end, and their purpose is to stop ants and other starving

souls from getting their mitts on them. Caddisfly larvae spin silken trapping nets in streams, which they use to capture small creatures for their dinner; the larvae of certain members of the mosquito family spin a trapping net that they use to gather up spores beneath fungi or to trap small insects. Some of these fungus gnat larvae are even luminous, emitting a blue-green light – although nobody has actually managed to explain why. Unlike the luminous mosquito larvae in the caves of New Zealand, which are predators and use the light to lure their food into the net, our European *Keroplatus* species seem content to obtain their protein from fungus spores and have no obvious reason to play at being light bulbs.

Among some species of dance flies the males use silk to pack up a delightful 'nuptial gift' for the female. The males are not predators themselves – they subsist peacefully on a diet of nectar – but they'll do anything for their greedy, protein-crazy inamorata so they trap an insect (preferably another male because that reduces the competition for females – two birds with one stone, so to speak) and wrap their prey up beautifully in silk produced by special glands on their forelegs. A suitor bearing gifts that he's even taken the trouble to package himself – it sounds delightful but the reality isn't especially romantic. This behaviour simply shows the hidden hand of evolution at work, as always. One theory is that the bigger the present and the better the packaging, the more time the male gets to mate. Consequently, he transmits more sperm and has a greater chance of passing on his genes. And it's fantastic for the female to receive a hefty dose of protein because laying eggs is an energy-intensive business.

But there's always the odd trickster who'll try to get the benefits without putting in the effort: some males give the female an empty ball of silk – and then have to get the mating over with pretty sharpish before the lady discovers she's been duped.

Weaving Miracles: The Spider's Silk

We can't talk about silk without mentioning spiders, even though they are arachnids rather than insects. The group takes its name from the person who became the first spider, according to Greek mythology: a talented weaver called Arachne, who had the temerity to challenge none other than Athene, the Greek goddess of war and wisdom, claiming to be the better weaver. The punishment for her arrogance was to be transformed into a spider. And what an ancestral mother Arachne turned out to be! Today, we know of more than 45,000 species of spiders. And the silk isn't just used to make webs for trapping the spider's prey, it is also a kind of compensation to the arachnids for lacking the wings they can only envy their distant relatives, the insects.

By climbing up to an airy spot and producing a long silken thread that the wind can catch, small spiders can sail away on the breeze using their own kiting technique.

Spider silk has impressive qualities. On a per-weight basis, it is six times stronger than steel, but at the same time highly elastic. That is why a heavy fly that blunders into the web can't simply pass straight through it. Instead, the web gives, a bit like the arresting cables that help fighter planes land on aircraft carriers. This enables thin fabric made of spider silk to halt a flying projectile – a property that can be used to make extremely light bulletproof vests, super-absorbent helmets and a new type of airbag for cars. If only we were able to learn how to get hold of sufficient amounts of spider silk ...

Experiments have shown that it is possible to harvest around 100 metres of silk from a single spider, but it's when you want to scale up that the trouble starts. Unlike the fat, laid-back silkworm larvae who think of nothing but eating the leaves of the mulberry tree and spinning their raw silk, spiders are predators who have no qualms about eating each other, so it's not especially easy to keep them in captivity in order to set up industrial-scale silk production.

A beautiful golden dress woven from the silk spun by golden orb spiders from Madagascar broke records for visitor numbers when exhibited in the Victoria and Albert Museum in London in 2012. And that's hardly surprising because it is a truly remarkable garment, which was four years in the making. Every morning, 80 workers collected new spiders. They were hooked up to a small hand-operated machine, where they were 'milked' of their silk and then released again in the evening. In all, 1.2 million spiders were needed.

It's plain to see that this is an unsustainable option for industrial production, so people have started to think along different lines. In 2002, the first 'spider goats' saw the light of day. With the aid of gene technology, scientists simply transferred 'spinning genes' from a spider to a goat, which then began to produce milk containing the proteins involved in silk production. This sparked considerable media attention but hasn't yet yielded any concrete results to speak of. Norway's neighbours have also thrown themselves into the race to produce synthetic spider silk. The Swedes recently reported that they had produced an entire kilometre of thread using water-soluble proteins produced by bacteria. The protein solution solidifies into spider silk when chemical conditions are altered – exactly the same thing that happens at the opening of the spider's spinnerets.

We're still a long way off commercial production and perhaps that's not so surprising: after all, spiders have had around 400 million years to perfect their silk.

Thank Insects for 700 Years of Notes

Shakespeare's plays and Beethoven's symphonies. Linnaeus's flower sketches and Galileo's drawings of the sun and the moon. Snorre's Sagas and the American Declaration of Independence. What do all these things have in common? They were all written using iron gall ink – a purplish-black ink that we have an insect to thank for. A tiny little insect called a gall wasp. These little critters are parasites on plants and trees, and are most commonly found on oaks. Gall wasps secrete a chemical substance that triggers a growth on the plant, which forms a house and pantry around one or several larvae.

There are many varieties of galls. One type that is often used for ink is the oak gall, also known as an oak apple. And it does, in fact, look like a small apple – perfectly round with a reddish tinge – except that it happens to be stuck to an oak leaf.

Inside their oak apples, gall wasp larvae lie chomping away on plant tissue in the peace and quiet, protected against all foes. Well, only partly, because some parasites have parasites of their own: unwelcome guests who turn up for dinner uninvited and refuse to leave again – such as guest gall wasps that simply move into other wasps' galls because they can't make their own. Worse still are the interlopers who use their long egg-laying stingers to poke their way through the walls of the gall and lay eggs in the very gall wasp larva living there. As a result, the insect that hatches out of a gall may be very different from the species responsible for the gall's creation in the first place.

The walls of the oak gall are stiff with a form of tannic acid. This acid occurs naturally in many plants and trees, and is the substance that links your leather jacket with a fine red wine. Tannic acid is crucial for tanning hides and leather, and at the same time, a master wine connoisseur can distinguish grape varieties and storage methods based on the tannins in a wine.

The first types of ink, made in China several thousand years before the Common Era, used carbon from lamp soot. The soot was mixed with water and gum arabic, a natural gum obtained from acacia trees, which kept the soot suspended in the liquid. But if you were unlucky enough to spill a cup of tea over your writing, your thoughts would be lost forever. Carbon ink was water-soluble and easy to wash away – which people also tended to do if they ran short of writing materials.

Later, people learnt to make ink from oak galls mixed with an iron salt and gum arabic. The great advantage of this new ink was that it was non-soluble: it ate its way into the parchment or paper that it was written on. What's more, it wasn't lumpy and was easy to make. From the 1100s to well into the 1800s, oak gall ink was the most commonly used variant in the Western world.

If it hadn't been for the little oak gall wasp it is far from certain that we would have so many well-preserved and legible documents from the great artists and scientists of the Middle Ages and the Renaissance. If we'd only had lampblack ink, many ancient thoughts, tunes and texts would have been washed away by water, either because storage conditions were poor or somebody wanted to re-use the parchment.

Carmine Red: Spaniards' Pride

Insects provide us with colours other than the brown-black hue of oak gall ink. They are also responsible for a beautiful, deep bright red colour that was, for several hundred years, exclusively produced in the Spanish colonies and which is still in use today, in both food and cosmetics.

Carmine dye is harvested from the females of a particular species of scale insect (*Dactylopius coccus*), peculiar creatures the size of a fingernail that are also known as cochineal bugs. Their natural habitat is in Southern and Central America, where the females spend their entire life on a single spot, wingless and firmly clamped beneath the protective shield of a prickly pear.

The dye was known to both the Aztecs and Mayans long

before the arrival of the Europeans, and they bred a variant that yielded a more intense red colour. Since this colour was both difficult and expensive to produce in Late Medieval Europe, dried cochineal bugs were one of the Spanish colonies' most important wares, valued on a par with silver – because carmine was an intense, powerful red colour that withstood sunlight without bleaching. The famous 'redcoats' of the British soldiers were dyed with carmine and Rembrandt, among others, used the colour in his paintings.

Since the dried insects were small and had no legs, and this was before the days of microscopes, Europeans were long uncertain whether the grains of carmine were animal, vegetable or mineral in origin. The Spaniards kept the secret close to their chests for nearly 200 years to assure their monopoly and the vast income the little insect generated for them.

Nowadays, carmine comes largely from Peru. The dye, whose E-number is E120, is used in many red food and beverage products, such as strawberry jam, Campari, yoghurt, juice, sauces and red sweets. You will also find it in different cosmetics, such as lipstick and eye shadow.

Shellac: From Varnish to False Teeth

What do jelly beans, gramophone records, violins and apples all have in common? A substance extracted from an insect, of course. It's a product with an incredible number of applications, yet you'll probably never have heard about its origins. We are talking about shellac, a resin-like substance produced by the lac bug (a relative of the cochineal bug that gives us carmine). There are heaps of these tiddlers on the branches of various tree species in Southeast Asia. According to some sources, the name derives from the Sanskrit word *lakh*, meaning 100,000, and refers to the enormous numbers of these bugs that can be found in a single place. (A brief diversion: the same source has it that the Norwegian word for salmon, *laks*, has the same linguistic origin for the same reason, because of the large amounts of salmon that gather in the mating season.)

There are several species of lac bugs, but the most common 'productive' variety is *Kerria lacca*. Lac bugs are members of the true bug family (*see page 36*) and spend most of their lives with their snouts stuck into plants. A pretty dull existence, then. But good heavens, the things this little life has given us humans! One science article went so far as to say that 'Lac is one of the most valuable gifts of nature to man.'

The tradition of cultivating lac bugs goes back a long way. The insect is mentioned in Hindu documents from 1200 BCE and Pliny the Elder described it as 'amber from India' in writings dated 77 CE. But it wasn't until the end of the 1300s that Europeans set their eyes on the product

– first as a dye and later as a varnish – in other words, a substance you apply to wood to form a glossy, waterproof surface. Beautiful furniture, woodwork and violins were all traditionally treated with shellac.

But it turned out to have many more areas of application. For 50 years, from the end of the 1800s right up until the 1940s, shellac was the main ingredient in gramophone records. It was mixed with ground rock and cotton fibre to produce what Norwegians used to call '*steinkaker*' or 'stone cakes': brittle, breakable 78 records (in other words, discs that rotated at 78 revolutions per minute). The sound reproduction was so-so but the early record players – or 'talking machines' as they were then known – were tremendous fun in those days. Bear in mind that radio hadn't yet become common: the world's first ever public radio broadcast wasn't transmitted until 1910 in New York City, and in Norway, test broadcasts didn't start until 1923, so for a long time gramophone records offered the only opportunity to host a 'virtual' orchestra or band in your own living room.

Record production was at such high levels in the 1900s that the American authorities started to get worried, because shellac was also important for the military industry, which used it in detonators and as a waterproof sealant for ammunition, among other applications. In 1942, the US authorities ordered the record industry to reduce its shellac consumption by 70 per cent.

But how do these tiny insects produce a substance with so many varied areas of application: in varnish, paint, glazing, jewellery and textile dyes, false teeth and fillings, cosmetics, perfume, electrical insulation, sealant, the glue used to restore dinosaur bones and a raft of other areas in the food and pharmaceutical industries?

It all starts with thousands of tiny lac bug nymphs settling on a suitable twig. With their sucking mouths, they slurp down plant sap; this undergoes a chemical change inside them and oozes out at the rear as an orange resin-like liquid, which hardens when it comes into contact with air. This forms small, shiny orange 'rooftops', which initially cover only the individual bugs, but gradually merge into one giant roof that shelters the entire colony and can cover a whole branch. After shedding their skins a few times, adult scale insects hatch out, then mate and lay eggs, well protected by the roof. The adults then die and the eggs hatch into thousands of new nymphs, which break through the resin roof and set off to find themselves a suitable new branch.

In order to make shellac, the resin coating must be scraped off the branches. It is then crushed and cleaned of insect fragments after which it is ready for market – as small amber-coloured flakes or dissolved in alcohol.

Most shellac production happens in India these days. And the good thing is that small-scale farmers in rural villages are the ones doing the job. Some three to four million people – many of whom have few other means of earning money – are estimated to earn their bread from keeping lac bugs as livestock. Moreover, the production helps keep species diversity rich in the 'grazing areas' of this tiny domestic creature. One reason for this is that little or no pesticide is used because that would also put the lac bugs' lives at risk.

Lac Bugs' Skincare Clinic for Dull Apples

Don't those shiny apples in the fruit aisles look delicious? Hardly surprising, because they've been for a waxing session at the lac bug's skincare clinic. What happens is this: we humans eliminate the apples' natural wax coating when we wash them after harvesting. And without wax, the apples quickly turn into wrinkly, unappetising fare that few people would want to sell and even fewer would wish to buy. So, apples have to be waxed again – and that's where shellac comes in, like a sort of anti-wrinkle cream.

Many other types of fruit and vegetables also undergo a round of shellacking to ensure that they last longer and look more appealing. The substance is approved for use on citrus fruits, melons, pears, peaches, pineapples, pomegranates, mangos, avocados, papayas and nuts. In 2013, shellac was also approved to buff up hens' eggs in Norway. The idea is to make the eggs nice and shiny, and increase their shelf life.

In the guise of E-number E904, shellac also turns up as glazing for various sweets, such as jelly beans, sugar-coated chocolates, pastilles and the like. This glazing agent goes by many other names: lacca, lac resin, gum lack, candy glaze or confectioner's glaze.

Shellac is used in cosmetics, too: in hairspray and nail varnish, and as a binding agent in mascara. It is also used in pills in capsule form, and not just to make the surface shiny: because shellac doesn't dissolve very easily in acid, it can be used to make 'delayed-release' pills. In other words, capsules that only dissolve when they reach the gut system.

Once you realise just how many strange places this product pops up in, perhaps it no longer seems so peculiar that somebody should call shellac one of the most valuable gifts of nature to man.

CHAPTER 8

Lifesavers, Pioneers and Nobel Prize-winners: Insights from Insects

Velcro is a genius invention. We use it on trainers and jackets, children's mittens and ski ties. It all started with a Swiss engineer who was out hunting with his dog and got annoyed because the mutt ended up covered in burrs every time they came home. That prompted him to take a closer look at those ingenious seed-dispersal mechanisms: small hooks that grab hold of passing animal pelts. *Hmm ... perhaps it was an idea worth copying?* And that's how Velcro came to be.

Engineers and designers are increasingly turning to natural solutions for inspiration. Nature has had billions of years to refine its solutions, and evolution has come up with countless smart structures and functions.

When it comes to shrewd solutions, insects make a strong showing because there are so many of them and they are so good at adapting. We can use them as model organisms, as we do with fruit flies (*see page 194*). We can make them do things for us that we can't do for ourselves, like crawl into collapsed buildings or help us to break down plastic. Perhaps they can provide us with new solutions to the antibiotics crisis, improve mental health among the population or even help make intergalactic travel possible. One thing is for certain: we'll be drawing inspiration from them and imitating them for a long time to come.

Biomimicry: Mother Nature Knows Best

According to the *Oxford English Dictionary*, biomimicry is 'the design and production of materials, structures and systems that are modelled on biological entities and processes'. There are numerous examples of biomimicry that started with insects. Dragonflies provide the inspiration for drone technology, while black fire beetles, which have heat sensors on their bellies – they lay their eggs in the embers of forest fires – are currently being studied by the US Army and others with a view to developing better heat-seeking sensors.

One key discovery, which offers huge potential, is that in many cases, insects' colour is not the result of pigments, but of special structures on the surface that reflect certain wavelengths of light. The result is an intense metallic colour that shifts depending on the angle you view it from, as with the magnificent bright blue morpho butterfly found in the jungles of South and Central America. Knowledge of structural colours may help us create colours that do not fade, as well as improved solar panels and mobile phone screens, and new types of cloth, paint and cosmetics. Or even banknotes that cannot be forged.

Breathe on Your Banknotes

The beautiful longhorn beetle *Tmesisternus isabellae*, whose only known habitat is a tiny area of Indonesia, changes colour according to atmospheric humidity. When it is dry, the beetle is gold with dark green stripes. If the humidity increases, its golden colouring shifts to red. Chinese chemical scientists recently copied this trick, applying it to printing technology.

The scientists reckon their insect-inspired ink can be used to print banknotes that are impossible to forge. If you want to check whether your money is genuine, simply breathe on it to see if it changes colour. In this way, a unique and rare beetle is helping to combat forgery and swindling.

So, the only thing left to worry about then is keeping your banknotes in a safe, insect-proof place – especially in the south, where termites are liable to eat anything with even a speck of cellulose, including banknotes. Termites in India have, in fact, chewed their way through fortunes on several occasions. In 2008, they chomped up all the spare cash an Indian businessman was keeping in the village bank, and in 2011, they munched through piles of rupee bills in a bank vault. The total value was well over a £100,000.

Termite Technology Creates Energy-saving Tower Blocks

Perhaps we can forgive termites for eating a few rupees here and there after all, once we see how much money we can save by copying their architectural solutions. You see, termites have given us some excellent ideas for improving energy efficiency in tall buildings by developing a more natural air-conditioning system.

The enormous termite mounds of Africa can tower several metres above the ground, housing millions of white or pale brown social individuals. Despite the baking heat outside, it is always pleasantly temperate inside the mound. And down in the depths, maybe a metre below the surface, Her Majesty the Queen of Termites lies in her perfectly temperate, oxygen-rich throne room, squeezing out eggs at a rate of knots. All around her, thousands of workers tend the fungus gardens that are like the mound's industrial kitchen (*see page 96*), where food is prepared for millions.

But the fungus is picky and only thrives in temperatures pretty close to 30°C: no more and no less. How do the termites manage to keep the interior temperature constant?

It turns out that an ingenious system of air channels uses temperature oscillations outside the mound over the course of the day and night to create a draught that runs through the construction. This 'artificial lung' ensures that cool, oxygen-rich air is drawn down, while warmer air, rich in carbon dioxide, is driven out.

Architects copied the termites' ingenious design when they built the Eastgate Centre, a large office and shopping complex in Harare. Although one of the largest malls in Zimbabwe, Eastgate doesn't have any regular air conditioning or heating. Instead, it uses passive cooling, applying the principles used by termites. As a result, the building uses only 10 per cent of the energy that would be consumed by an equivalent building with standard mechanised air-con systems.

From Brown Bananas to Nobel Prizes

You're probably familiar with fruit flies, those sluggish so-and-sos that form a whole cloud when they fly up off your fruit. Irritating as they may be, these tiny red-eyed critters are, in fact, the owners of no fewer than six Nobel Prizes.

Their family name in Latin is *Drosophila*, 'one who loves the morning dew', which sounds a lot more poetic than 'fruit fly' and reflects the fact that these insects originally inhabited warm and humid tropical climes. Today, many of the species in the fruit-fly family are found throughout the world (with the exception of Antarctica). One common feature of the species that is liable to turn up uninvited in UK kitchens is that they thrive on rotting, fermenting organic stuff, such as compost, over-ripe fruit or the dregs in the bottom of a beer can. There, they lay their eggs and develop at record rates.

Of course, they are pretty annoying – we'd much rather insects left our food alone and stuck to the outdoor life. But these flitting critters are actually more important than you might think. Indeed, the *Drosophila melanogaster* fruit fly is the uncrowned King of the Laboratory, having been a crucial component of research and lab experiments for more than 100 years.

Fruit flies have masses of excellent traits that make them particularly suitable for research: they are cheap and easy to keep in laboratories, live at a supersonic pace and have oodles of offspring too. What's more, we have a good grasp of the species' genetic material or DNA, having fully mapped its genome in 2000. Without wishing to insult anybody, I can reveal that human genes are more akin to those of a fruit fly than we might like. For example, one study that examined a selection of disease-related gene sequences in humans found that 77 per cent of them also occurred in fruit flies. It is precisely this similarity that makes fruit-fly research such a useful way of understanding various phenomena, even in human beings. The flies have taught us a lot about chromosomes and the way that traits are transmitted. This earned Thomas Hunt Morgan a Nobel Prize in 1933. Thirteen years later, after being fried with massive doses of radiation, the fly and Hermann Müller won another Nobel Prize (in 1946) for showing that radiation leads to mutations and causes genetic damage. In 1995, the Nobel Prize for medicine and physiology once again went to our wee winged pal, along with a three-strong team whose wide-ranging work showed how genes control development in the early stages of foetal life. Then in 2004, the prize went to research on the fly's system of smell, and in 2011, to work on its immune defences. In 2017, the fly won its last Nobel – to date – this time for studies into the built-in clock that controls the circadian rhythm of living organisms. These last prizes are particularly good examples of fly research that is highly transferrable to us humans.

Even the thing we find most annoying about the fly – its attraction to stuff that is fermenting and preferably contains alcohol – has turned out to be useful. The research into 'alcoholism' in fruit flies is a serious and important business, but also involves plenty of human parallels that are sure to pep up the conversation at Oktoberfest. Like the fact that excess alcohol makes male flies clingy and sex-mad, while simultaneously reducing their chances of successful mating. Or that when male flies lose out on the dating market, they 'drown their sorrows' by drinking more than their rivals who have managed to mate successfully.

As if that weren't enough, fruit flies continue to increase our knowledge of diseases such as cancer and Parkinson's, as well as phenomena like insomnia and jetlag, so a bit of respect might be in order next time you catch yourself cursing those tiny flies in your kitchen. As you set up a suitable fruit-fly trap, maybe you can at least whisper a small thank-you to one of the most important creatures in biomedical research.

Ants Give Us New Antibiotics

Bacteria are increasingly developing resistance to antibiotics – a large and growing problem. According to the World Health Organization, this causes more than 700,000 deaths every year. Knowledge of ecology and evolution is a crucial tool in the battle against antibiotic resistance, and insects are contributing to the solutions.

Ants are an especially interesting subject of study.

They live close together in large societies and need good defences against bacteria and fungi to prevent the death of the entire colony. That is why ants have two special glands on their bodies that produce antibiotics. They smear it over themselves and their sisters using their forelegs, and experiments have shown that this activity increases when fungus spores are present in the nest.

Leaf-cutter ants – the ones who take home leaves, which they chew up and use as a base for cultivating fungi (*see page 94*) – face extra challenges when it comes to fungal infections: other parasitic fungi sometimes try to establish themselves in the ants' fungus gardens. If successful, they can kill both the fungus crops and the ants themselves, so the ants have developed a powerful defence against such invaders: a collaboration with bacteria that live in special pouches on the ant's body and produce a type of antibiotic that kills the fungal invaders. It is a finely tuned collaboration that has been perfected over millions of years. Studies of this cooperation between ants and bacteria therefore offer us good opportunities to identify effective ways of killing fungi and bacteria. Several discoveries have already been patented, including a fungicidal antibiotic from leaf-cutter ants called Selvamicin, which is effective against yeast infections by *Candida albicans*, a fungus many of us have encountered in the form of oral or genital infections.

Larval Therapy

I'm always happy to see clothes or jewellery with insect motifs. It doesn't happen all that frequently, although a beautiful butterfly or a fluffy bumblebee can often now be seen on garments or iconic pieces of jewellery. But flies? Rarely. I carried out a small, extremely unscientific test: an internet search for 'butterfly jewellery' in Norwegian resulted in around 1,000 hits. If I switched 'butterfly' for 'blow fly', I didn't get a single hit.

We think of blow flies as vectors of disease, but these insects can actually heal us by feeding off our infected wounds. It sounds revolting but this is old news: Genghis Khan was a thirteenth-century Mongolian warlord who founded the empire deemed to be the largest by area in the history of the world, stretching from Korea to Poland. And he didn't create this kingdom through diplomacy and negotiations, either, but exclusively through brutal and ruthless warfare. Legend has it that he always took a wagon full of maggots into battle with him. They were placed on his soldiers' wounds, which made them heal better so that the men could be sent back to the battle-field more quickly.

This kind of larval therapy was also used with great success during the Napoleonic Wars, the American Civil War and the First World War. After we discovered the fantastic properties of antibiotics, larval therapy sank into oblivion. More recently, though, it has returned to the fore, largely because of multi-drug-resistant bacteria.

The larvae of the common green bottle, *Lucilia sericata*, are the ones most commonly used for this purpose. This fly can be found outdoors throughout the United Kingdom. When used for medical purposes it is critical for the maggots to be sterile before they are placed on the wound, so they are bred in special laboratories. The maggots are often placed in a kind of coarse-mesh teabag to ensure that they can't escape but are still able to stick their heads through the mesh to get their job done. And their job involves multitasking: the larvae limit the growth of the bacteria in the wound by producing antibiotic-like substances, and substances that alter the pH value of the wound. Also, they simply eat up the dead wound tissue. In some cases, they have been found to produce substances that promote the growth of new tissue. They eat only dead tissue and pus, and do not touch the living tissue around the wound.

One of the more creative experiments involving blow flies was conducted in the early 1900s by the Maggot King, an Englishman who believed it was wholesome and healthy for humans to inhale the vapours of fly larvae. This chap had tuberculosis, but was convinced that the maggots he bred as bait for his frequent fishing trips were what kept him alive and he was eager to share this knowledge with other sufferers, so every summer the Maggot King had several tonnes of dead animals sent to him, generally from zoos. He would leave them outdoors until they were full of maggots, which he harvested and transferred to special containers, and then placed indoors in what he called maggotoriums. These were wooden shacks where the patients could sit among the containers of maggots and stinking rotten meat, entertaining themselves with a book, a hand of cards or a friendly chat with the other invalids.

I'm sure few readers if any will be surprised to learn that this business idea really stank! People could smell the stench of the Maggot King's farm for miles around and his views garnered little scientific support. Although several patients testified that their health had improved after spending time among the rotting animals, the inhalation of maggot gases never became a commercial success. But maybe the future will show that the Maggot King was not entirely on the wrong track. Blow-fly larvae can apparently produce gaseous emissions that limit the growth of a non-pathogenic relative of the tuberculosis bacterium often used as a test organism. Pending further research, those who use live bait for fishing might as well draw an extra-deep breath over their maggot tins purely for the sake of their health.

Crickets as Pets

Insects can also help our mental health. It is common knowledge that keeping pets can improve your happiness and health, and in the East, people have kept insects as pets for thousands of years. In China and Japan, in particular, they have often kept caged crickets, relatives of the grasshopper. The primary attraction was their beautiful song, but in thirteenth-century China, it was also popular to arrange cricket fights. Indeed, an annual two-day cricket-fighting championship is still held in China to this day. And it is just one of more than 100 traditional Chinese festivals associated with insects.

It is not an uncommon hobby among Japanese children to catch (or, if they live in a town, buy) large male beetles and arrange fights between them. We're talking about some of the planet's largest beetle species here, with powerful horns or long mandibles, which the males use to fight. In Japan, as in the US, popular bus tours are also laid on so that people can see fireflies (which are beetles, not flies) dancing in the night at special locations.

Now, insect pets are being tested out as a modern method of geriatric care – in Asia, of course. Because what happens if elderly Koreans have a cage full of crickets placed in their charge?

Nearly 100 Koreans with a mean age of 71 were tested

for psychological factors such as depression, anxiety, stress levels, sleeping difficulties and quality of life. After that, they were divided evenly into two groups. While both groups received guidance on healthy living and weekly follow-up phone calls, only half of the subjects were given a cage that contained five chirping crickets. The species in question was *Teleogryllus mitratus* – a garden cricket that lives in Southeast Asia, whose 'song' is considered extremely beautiful and pleasing to the ear.

After two months, all the participants were interviewed and tested again. Almost all the old people liked their crickets, and three-quarters of them felt that caring for the insects had improved their mental health. The test results also showed a slightly positive effect on several of the factors that were measured; in particular, a reduced level of depression and an improvement in quality of life.

The good thing about a cricket in a cage is that it is cheap to buy and needs little looking after – the old people don't have to take them out for air, clip their claws or groom their coats, yet it can be rewarding for them to watch the cricket shuffle around in its cage and sing, and it needs a spot of food from time to time. In fact, it needs you, which is good to know. Caring for a cricket can be the little bonus that gives daily life some meaning for those in poor physical health, who can't do much, and spend a lot of time sitting alone.

Biophilia – Love of Nature

Fortunately, it seems as if interest in insects is also growing in the West. Many people have become aware of buzzing bees and chubby bumblebees. They are planting nectar-rich flowers, hanging up insect hotels (bird boxes, but for insects) and building bumblebee nest boxes in their gardens. Many insect-lovers are doing an important job by seeking out and collecting (or photographing) insects from new places. It's like a treasure hunt that offers rewarding experiences of nature while increasing our knowledge of insects.

In several places, particularly warmer climes, you can find butterfly houses, large areas enclosed in a net, where butterflies can fly around freely, being admired and photographed. One Norwegian nature photographer (Kjell Sandved, who works at a museum in Washington DC) has become world famous for his butterfly alphabet – beautiful close-ups of butterfly wings displaying letters. The overwintering habitats of the monarch butterfly in Mexico draw tourists from all over the globe, and in 2016, half a million people visited New Zealand to admire the luminous fungus gnat larvae in the ceiling of the Waitomo Caves.

These phenomena highlight an issue that concerned the famous insect scientist, Edward O. Wilson: the need we humans have for a deep and intimate connection to nature and other species. Wilson called it biophilia – the love of living things. He believed it was a trait that had developed and been reinforced throughout our evolution because it increased our chances of survival to be in close contact with nature. If you paid attention to the flowers, you could find their fruit a few weeks later. And if you were familiar with the species that might harm you or kill you, your chances of survival rose. Many are of the view that our suspicion of snakes and spiders can be traced back to this kind of adaptation.

Nowadays, ever more research confirms how important it is for human health and wellbeing to be close to nature. Older people survive longer if they live close to a green area, regardless of socioeconomic status. Students learn better if they can see a patch of green outside their window. Children with personality disorders have fewer symptoms after pursuing activities in nature. It was found that when people moved into social housing and were randomly distributed between housing with green areas and housing whose outside areas were tarmacked over, those in housing with green outer areas experienced less violence in the home.

When my children were in infants' school, I got to join them on trips to the stream in springtime. Sceptical 10-year-olds would watch me use a metal sieve on a long pole to fish up brown mud, which I would tip out onto a white plastic tray on the ground.

'Yuck! You're not going to touch that, are you?' somebody whines. But then the miracle happens: the mud settles and teeming life emerges. Together, we gaze at whirligig beetles with two pairs of eyes – that allow them to see clearly both above and below water – and talk about how the silver bubble on the rear end of another beetle is an air bubble that it's breathing in.

Suddenly, there's a battle for the plastic tray and the sieve. Everybody wants to find the strange bugs. Forgotten are the cloth shoes that won't withstand the water, forgotten is their fear of getting mud beneath their varnished nails.

These days have left me with good memories, filled with an intense sense of having contributed to something meaningful.

More than half of the world's population now lives in cities and the numbers will only increase. Many lack opportunities to visit wilderness areas or have close encounters with wild animals. Luckily, local wild-flower areas and urban green spaces can be excellent examples of the natural world and you're guaranteed to find insects there.

Cockroaches: Humanity's Best Friend?

New ways of living create new problems and subsequently new opportunities for making use of insects. Rescue work in cities, for example in a collapsed building, presents very particular challenges. St Bernard dogs with casks beneath their chins can't help us here. In the modern-day urban environment your guardian angel may soon turn out to be a cockroach.

You've probably heard the saying that cockroaches are the only things that will survive a nuclear war. It's a myth spawned by old films with thrilling titles like *Them!*, *Bug* or *Twilight of the Cockroaches*; films dominated by post-apocalyptic monster insects that eat atomic fallout for breakfast and any surviving women – preferably red-frocked beauties – for dessert. It's nonsense, of course, although it is true that cockroaches can withstand more radioactivity than us humans (by the way, mealworm beetles can withstand even more).

Cockroaches' resilience, not to mention their robust physique and spectacular motor skills, can actually be useful to us humans. Pack a small cockroach rucksack full of modern technology: a microchip, a transmitter and receiver, and a control unit that is connected to the cockroach's antennae and cerci – the tactile, tail-like appendages on its rear end. The micro-controller, which is operated remotely, can stimulate the cerci with small electric impulses. This makes the cockroach think that something is approaching it from behind and so it runs away. If you send an impulse to an antenna, the cockroach thinks it has touched something and nimbly turns aside. In this way, you can remotely steer a whole armada of rucksack-bearing cockroaches through a dangerous building and, by interpreting the signals sent back, you can draw a map of the accident site.

The rucksack can also be supplemented with a microphone that captures audio in the surrounding areas. In this way, the people remotely controlling the cockroach can listen out for sounds from those who are trapped – after an earthquake, say. By steering the cockroach towards the sound, they can identify the position and come to the rescue more speedily.

So, if you should be unlucky enough to become trapped in a collapsed building, don't be too quick to stamp on any cockroaches that happen to come your way: they may prove to be your salvation. If, on the other hand, you should become lost in the Swiss Alps on a winter's day, you'd be better off pinning your hopes on a St Bernard – snowy weather is one of the few things a cockroach can't deal with.

Plastic on the Menu

Every minute enough plastic is dumped into the world's oceans to fill an entire bin lorry. At least as much again ends up in landfill sites and the amounts are constantly increasing. Because we love plastic: it's handy and cheap. We produce and use 20 times more plastic every year now than we did 50 years ago, and less than 10 per cent of it gets recycled, although, luckily, the focus on reducing plastic use is increasing. The rest of the plastic waste ends up in landfill, in roadside ditches or in the sea. A report issued by the Ellen MacArthur Foundation estimates that if this continues, the sea will contain more plastic than fish by 2050. This is because plastic biodegrades extremely slowly in the natural environment, so the discovery that a number of insects can digest and break down plastic is something of a sensation.

Take polystyrene, for example. Even if you don't think you use it that often, I'm guessing you've held some in your hand – if you've ever bought takeaway food in a carton or a hot drink in anything other than a paper cup. Because polystyrene (also known as isopore) is the material used to make disposable containers for hot food and drink. In the US alone, 2.5 billion such cups are thrown away every year – and we're talking about a material that was thought to be non-biodegradable – until now, that is. It turns out that mealworms scoff down isopore cups as if they were part of their regular diet.

Several hundred American and Chinese mealworms were served some isopore. All of them belonged to the darkling beetle species (*Tenebrio molitor*), which lives outdoors all across Europe and sometimes turns up indoors too, if any soggy flour residue is left lying in your cupboards for too long. They gobbled up the isopore at record speed and the larvae raised on this peculiar diet pupated and hatched into adult beetles as normal. Within a month, for example, 500 Chinese mealworms had gobbled up a third of the 5.8 grams of isopore served up to them. All that was left was some carbon dioxide and a spot of beetle poo, which was apparently pure enough to use as planting soil. There was no difference between the survival rates of larvae that received normal food and those on the isopore diet.

But this can hardly be called a superfood. So, another experiment compared three different groups: larvae that received isopore, larvae that received some kind of cornflakes and larvae that received no food at all. The weight of the cornflake larvae increased by 36 per cent while the isopore larvae didn't put on any weight. But they still did better than the poor starving souls, who lost a quarter of their weight over the two-week duration of the experiment.

Strictly speaking, the beetles themselves aren't the ones doing the job of breaking down the plastic. For this they rely on some delightful tenants in their gut. If the mealworms are given antibiotics that kill off this gut flora, their ability to break down plastic also vanishes. The breakdown of plastic probably depends on the combined efforts of both beetle and bacteria.

More research needs to be done into whether this can help us solve the problem of plastic in the oceans because mealworm beetles aren't keen on getting their feet wet and are hardly suited to the seagoing life. But there is plenty of plastic on dry land that we'd love to get rid of, and these beetles may be able to help.

And mealworms are not alone. Other insects can also help solve the plastic problem. The greater wax moth is a Lepidopteran that is viewed as a pest by beekeepers because it eats the wax combs inside beehives. But beeswax has a similar structure to polyethylene, which is the kind of plastic used in supermarket shopping bags – and sure enough, it turns out that the wax moth can eat holes in this kind of plastic and transform it into ethylene glycol, a substance we know as antifreeze for use in cars. Again, this task is not down to the larva alone, but probably a result of bacteria living inside its gut.

Now, researchers are poring over these recent findings to discover how we can mass-produce the active substances and perhaps, over the long term, translate this into a practical solution to help us deal with our plastic waste.

Forever Young: The Beetle with the Elixir of Youth

Sometimes scientific discoveries come about quite by chance, like when an American scientist happened to forget some larvae in a drawer around the end of the First World War. It's probably easy to get in a muddle when, like this chap, you're studying everything from human cell structures and causes of sterility in mules to the caddisfly's reaction to light. But quite *why* this scientist happened to leave a tin of beetle larvae in his office drawer in the first place is a mystery.

At any rate, the point is not that he left them there but that he forgot about them. Totally and absolutely – for five whole months. And for a carpet beetle like *Trogoderma glabrum*, whose normal life cycle is a mere two months from tiny egg to dead adult beetle, five months without food should have been the end. But when the scientist finally rediscovered the larvae in his drawer, he found them in the best of health. Stranger still, they had grown younger! Yes, they really had!

If you cast your mind back to the first chapter, with its crash course in insect lore, you may remember that all insects shed their skin a number of times en route to adulthood (*see page 4*). This is normally meant to go one way and one way only: from tiny larva to larger and more developed larva – just as we humans can only go from baby to teenager and not the reverse. But the larvae in the drawer had, in fact, gone the opposite way: they had developed backwards, from big to little – from an advanced to a simpler larval stage.

This was revolutionary stuff. Our friend grasped that much. He continued to starve the beetle larvae and discovered that these crazy critters could stay alive for more than five years 'without a particle to eat', as he wrote. They simply got smaller and smaller because they were *living their lives backwards* – going from the late larval stages to the very earliest. Stranger still, when these poor wretches on enforced hunger strike were given access to food once more, the switch flipped back to normal mode and the development from 'baby' to 'youth' resumed.

A slightly more recent study from the 1970s confirms these old findings. The larvae of the *Trogoderma glabrum* can develop forwards and backwards repeatedly. True, the process is not entirely without cost because although it may look like a 'baby larva', a larva that has undergone repeated back-and-forth cycles will display physiological deterioration, indicating that it has aged after all. With each new round, it takes longer for the larva to grow bigger again.

It's a pretty wild business! And there's more where that comes from: the ageing process can also be controlled in honeybees. Bees that are responsible for looking after the young in the hive can live and remain at the height of their mental powers for many weeks. However, worker bees – the ones that go out and gather nectar – die, thoroughly senile, after a couple of weeks. The ingenious thing is that if worker bees are forced to take on the hive bees' job again, some of them actually 'grow younger' – they recover a longer life with high mental capacity. In honeybees, this is controlled by a special protein, a kind of elixir of youth especially for bees. Studies of these insects can help us to understand the ageing processes in humans too, which may lead to new insights in areas such as dementia-related diseases, ultimately helping us to achieve better health in our old age.

Midges in Space

Speaking of life expectancy and ageing, how about a trick that could help us with interstellar travel? Perhaps insects can help there too. A non-biting midge known as the sleeping chironomid, *Polypedilum vanderplanki*, is actually a hard-core aspiring astronaut equipped for prolonged periods of sleep.

The midge lives in Africa and the larva spends its life in small puddles of water that are constantly drying out. But whereas we humans die if we lose more than 14 per cent of the water in our bodies, and most other organisms can only withstand a maximum water loss of 50 per cent, this creature can cope with a loss of up to 97 per cent! In this desiccated state, the larvae can handle pretty much any pummelling: you can boil them, dip them in liquid nitrogen, soak them in spirit, expose them to cosmic radiation for years, or simply leave them alone; the record survival time is 17 years to date.

When it is time for them to wake up, all you have to do is pour water on them and – hey presto! – like those freeze-dried chunks of meat in packet soup, the midge larvae swell up to their normal size. Give it an hour, and they will be busy eating again as if nothing has happened.

So, the midge larva can enter into a state that is somewhere between life and death without suffering any apparent harm. All it needs is a little time to prepare itself. Because the key to survival seems to be for it to replace the water in its body with a kind of sugar called trehalose. This sugar is only about half as sweet as normal sugar and occurs naturally in small concentrations in insect blood. Incidentally, trehalose is named after the cocoon-shaped larval secretions of a true weevil (or snout beetle) found in Iran, which is known as *trehala* in Persian and widely used in Persian traditional medicine.

When the midge realises that tough times lie ahead its body begins to produce more trehalose sugar, which rises from the normal level of around 1 per cent of its blood up to around 20 per cent. The sugar protects the cells and bodily functions in various ways.

Several other organisms have mastered the art of becoming the living dead, including bacteria, fungi (think of dried yeast!), roundworms, tardigrades and springtails.

The exciting thing is that they don't all use the same techniques. In tardigrades, for example, there is no sign of trehalose accumulation.

If we can get to the bottom of the processes that control this switch between normal life and desiccated dormancy, we can use this information to keep cells, tissue or perhaps even individuals in a desiccated state. Perhaps an African midge will help us find the key to interstellar travel in the future.

Robot Bees

While we wait for insects to help us travel to the stars, how about getting them to help us travel among the flowers in the meantime? That way, they can pollinate plants for us along the way. Because robot bees do actually exist, in laboratories, at any rate: tiny drones that have been pimped up with a brush and electrically charged gel so that they can gather pollen. Carbon-fibre brushes, nylon hair from a make-up brush (yes, really) and horsehair were all tested out, and although horses aren't known for their pollinating skills, the horsehair brush still turned out to work best. With that, robot bee 1.0 was ready for testing. You can find a video clip on the Internet of the drone flying from lily to lily in the Japanese laboratory where it was created. The flight itself is rather clumsy, but then again, drone flying isn't on the university curriculum – yet.

The most obvious area of application for these sorts of drones is on pollination-dependent food crops in green-houses. This might allow us to restrict the use of intro-duced bumblebee species, which have a habit of escaping the greenhouses and dispersing in the natural world. For now, the robot bees aren't especially efficient because they have to be controlled manually and need constant recharg-ing, but perhaps in the future they will be able to navigate using GPS or be controlled by artificial intelligence, and will have batteries with a longer life.

But let's hope we don't end up in a world where we believe modern mechanics can replace nature's infinite advanced functions. In nature, more than 20,000 different species contribute to the pollination of wild flowers and crops, and research shows that pollination is most effective when a diverse range of species with different special adap-tations is involved. We know that the interplay between insects and flowers has been fine-tuned over more than 100 million years, and that natural pollination is far more complex and ingenious than any imitation we might come up with. It is simply easier and cheaper to conserve the solutions that nature gives us free of charge.

And when it comes to gaining new insights from old insects, we never know which species will turn out to be useful next: mealworms, fruit flies or cockroaches; ants or midges? We humans are quick to categorise other species according to whether they are a help or hindrance to us and we're generally keen to get rid of the ones that fall into the latter group, but nature is so cleverly organised that, with better knowledge, we will always be discovering new smart solutions out there. That is one reason why it is so important to conserve the natural world and all the species living in it, whether we consider them useful or not.

CHAPTER 9

Insects and Us: What's Next?

The extraordinary lives of insects are changing; the ecosystems on Earth have altered more rapidly in the past hundred years than at any previous time in human history. Well over half of the planet's land area has been transformed through agriculture, livestock grazing and construction. And the pace is increasing. This means that habitats are being lost and those that remain are being divided into small, isolated fragments. Dams and artificial irrigation are putting the planet's freshwater resources under ever-increasing pressure. We have produced and thrown away so much plastic that we will be finding vestiges of it in the sediments in the form of microplastic for generations to come. Every year, we produce substantial amounts of chemicals, including the pesticides we use to protect our crops, which in turn kill insects. We displace species, both intentionally and unintentionally. We have doubled the amount of nitrogen and phosphorus in the soil through the use of artificial fertiliser, and CO_2 emissions are higher than they have been for tens of millions of years, contributing to climate change.

All of this affects insects – and anything that affects insects affects us. Indeed, a decline in the number of insects and the extinction of species will spread through the ecosystem in a ripple effect with major consequences over time because of the impact on so many fundamental ecological functions. Fortunately, we'll never manage to wipe out all the bugs, but we would do well to take more care of our tiny, six-legged, winged friends, because despite their 479-million-year track record, they're starting to struggle.

We only know of a tiny proportion of all the insect species in existence, and we have little solid monitoring data about those we do know of. Even so, one estimate indicates that a quarter of all insects may be under threat of extinction.

One important point in this connection: it's too late to worry when a species is on the brink of extinction. Species cease to function in the ecosystem long before the last individual dies out. That is why it is so vital not to focus exclusively on species extinction, but also to turn the spotlight on the decline in the number of individuals, and there is much to suggest that insects are becoming fewer. In Germany, the accumulated biomass of all insects trapped in more than 60 locations nationwide has plummeted 75 per cent in just 30 years. Global data suggests that while we humans have doubled our population in the past 40 years, the number of insects has been reduced by almost half – these are dramatic figures.

So, why are insect numbers falling? It's not so easy to say because there are almost certainly many connected causes. Important factors include increasing land use, intensive farming and forestry practices, pesticides and the decline in natural remnant habitats, as well as climate change.

What happens when our demands for constant growth in the use of land and resources cause insect populations to crash, species to disappear and insect communities to change? Think of the world as a hammock made of woven fabric: all the species on the planet and their lives form part of the weaving and all of them combined create the hammock we humans are resting in. Insects are so numerous that they account for a large share of the hammock's fabric. If we reduce insect populations and wipe out insect species, it's as if we are pulling threads out of this weaving. That might be fine as long as there are only a few small holes and loose threads here and there, but if we pull out too many threads, the whole hammock will eventually unravel – and our welfare and wellbeing along with it.

Overly drastic changes in insect communities can have domino effects with consequences nobody can predict.

Indeed, we do not know what their significance might be – only that things may become very different. We risk living in a world where we humans face a tougher existence because the challenges of assuring clean water, sufficient food and good health for all become even greater than they are today.

In conclusion, let's look at a few challenges, some examples of the factors that threaten insect life, both locally and globally.

First, land use. This is undoubtedly the greatest threat. We are using land ever more intensively, which means fewer habitats and less intact rainforest in the tropics. Back home, fewer flower meadows in agricultural land and densely built-up areas, and fewer areas of natural forest, where old dead trees get to play out their role as housing estates for insect diversity. It also means more artificial light, which has an impact on many insects.

Second, climate change. Warmer, wetter, wilder – that's the outlook. And what do these changes mean for insect life?

Third, challenges related to the use of pesticides and new genetic manipulation techniques. A vast field that leaves us with more questions than answers.

Fourth, and finally, the introduction of non-native species and their effect on bugs. What is the right way of dealing with 'past sins' in this area? Is it possible to reverse them and is this the correct prioritisation? Because at the same time as we wipe out species, the changes we make also create room on the planet for new species, brought to the fore by the thrust of evolution. How robust is nature and how shall we weigh up concern for our own kind against concern for millions of other species?

The Frog You Wouldn't Want to Kiss

In the South American jungle lives a poisonous frog with the thoroughly appropriate Latin name of *Phyllobates terribilis*. In English, it goes by the name of golden poison frog. This isn't a frog you'd want to kiss in the hope of finding a handsome prince. If you tried, you'd be dead within minutes – guaranteed. The poison in question is one of the most powerful nerve poisons known to mankind, batrachotoxin. An average frog contains roughly 1 milligram of the poison – about the same weight as a grain of salt. This alone is enough to kill 10 grown men. And just so you know: there's no antidote.

This little frog, no larger than a plum, used to be fairly common in the rainforest in parts of Colombia. The locals would carefully stroke their arrows along the frog's back to ensure that their arrowhead was poisonous enough to kill anything they might encounter.

The pharmaceutical industry got wind of this shocking yellow poisonous sensation in the rainforest. Early tests indicated that the poison was an incredibly effective pain-killer – in suitable doses. What's more, because it affects the transportation of sodium through cell membranes, it could also be significant for our understanding of numerous diseases where this is important, such as multiple sclerosis (MS). A few specimens were fetched from the jungle for closer examination, but guess what happened to the catch when it arrived in the laboratory? The frog was no longer poisonous!

The fact is that nature is often craftier than we expect: the golden poison frog is not poisonous in itself, it only produces the poison while living in its natural habitat. Why? After much laborious detective work we now know that the poison comes from a diet of – yes, that's right (this is a book about insects after all) – beetles! A beetle from the soft-winged flower beetle family, Melyridae, to be precise. So, the frog is only poisonous when it gets to eat the right kind of beetles in its natural forest habitat.

Thanks to rainforest logging the golden poison frog is now listed as threatened with extinction. A desperate battle to rescue the species is under way, but there are few bright spots. Not only is the frog's habitat vanishing but the trade in frog legs has led to the spread of a fungal disease (popularly known as Bd), which is killing frogs, toads and newts across the globe. A third of them are now on the point of vanishing for good. Soon there will no longer be any golden poison frogs and no opportunity to do further research into the active ingredients they produce.

Varied Landscapes Increase Insect Numbers

If we want to preserve our chances of seeking out active medical ingredients, we need to take care of the habitats of these species. Conserving natural areas intact is one important means of securing habitats, both in the rainforest and here in Europe. Many specialised insects have such peculiar, special needs when it comes to where they can live that they cannot survive in a totally transformed modern landscape. This means that nature reserves and other conservation areas are crucial if we are to safeguard unique species. But it is also important to retain as much of the variation seen in the natural landscape in places outside the large conservation areas too. In the forest, that may mean ensuring there are enough old trees and dead trees. Because dead wood plays a central role in a living forest (*see page 139*), housing a large share of forest species, including insects – which make themselves useful as decomposers, pollinators, dispersers of seeds, as food for other animals and as pest controllers. And although many European countries have recently launched initiatives to increase the amount of dead wood, the volumes are still low compared to natural conditions.

In our farmland and cities we can also achieve a great deal through simple measures that simultaneously serve to beautify the environment for us humans: a belt of trees and bushes alongside a stream in a residential area; verge- and hedgerow-cutting along the roads and a border of wild-flower meadow along the edge of a field; a patch of uncultivated land in the middle of a field with old hollow oak trees. A varied landscape offers many more opportunities for complex insect life. Again, this benefits the pollination of both wild flowers and our crop plants. Because honeybees, wild bees and bumblebees aren't the only insects required for good and efficient pollination. This is high-level teamwork involving many players. It is often the case that flies, beetles, ants, wasps and butter-flies are less efficient pollinators *per flower visit* than bees and bumblebees, yet this is frequently offset by the fact that they visit many more flowers overall because there are a heck of a lot of them. Some of these 'non-bees' may also have peculiar habits and adaptations that benefit effective pollination.

If we combine data from a few dozen research proj-ects from five continents about crops of, say, rape, water-melon, mangoes, strawberries, and apples, we find that the plants produced better crops (an increased fruit set) when they received visits from 'non-bees' regardless of how many bees paid them a visit. It seems that these other insects contribute something unique, something that bees cannot deliver. There are also differences in how vulnerable the different insects are to changes in the landscape, which is an advantage for our food production. In sum, all these insects operate as a kind of pollinator insurance: if one species can't get the job done, another one can step in.

We know that intact species diversity can make the ecosystem more effective when it comes to capturing resources, such as water and nutrients, and this results in more biomass. That knowledge is key once we grasp that this biomass is precisely what serves as the basis for crops, and the food that ends up on our dinner table. We also know that species diversity is central to breaking down the biomass once again and thereby ensuring that the nutrients are released, which enables new production.

What's more, we are gaining increasing support for the notion that intact biological diversity can make ecosystems more stable over time than impoverished diversity. There are many mechanisms in play, including the fact that different species have different strengths. One species grows best during cool summers, while another shines beneath a baking summer sun. When species decline or are wiped out, nature has fewer variants to play with and we are more poorly armed against both natural fluctuations and man-made changes – in the climate, for example.

227

It's not easy to put a price on the services insects provide, although that hasn't stopped people from trying. For example, the annual global contribution of the many pollinating insects is estimated to be worth around $US 577 billion – equivalent to a little under two-thirds of UK current revenue for 2015. Decomposition and soil formation are estimated to be worth four times as much as pollination in total. Although these figures vary depending on calculation methods and are pretty approximate, they still show that the contribution from insects is extremely valuable in pounds, shillings and pence, and it makes good economic sense to look after them.

Troublesome Light

The fact that we humans are spreading out over increasingly larger expanses of the planet also has some consequences we don't think about on a day-to-day basis, such as light pollution – the sum of artificial outdoor light produced by streetlamps, houses, holiday cottages and industrial buildings. Light pollution is currently growing at a rate of 6 per cent per year and is disturbing our ecosystems, including insects.

We all know that moths are attracted to light, although the exact cause is a matter of debate. According to the leading theory, they think the light is the moon and try to orientate themselves by maintaining a fixed angle to it. While this works perfectly well with the moon, which is an awfully long way off, the result in this case is that they spiral in towards the artificial light and generally end up getting fried.

Street lighting can alter the local species composition of bugs. When artificial light is reflected off shiny surfaces, this can also confuse land-living insects that lay their eggs in water. Where we see a parked car beneath a streetlight, a dragonfly simply perceives the light as being reflected off the surface of a body of water, and drops its entire life's egg production in the wrong place.

And what happens to insects over the long term? Could light pollution cause urban insects to change their behaviour and avoid light, for example? To test this, some Swiss scientists compared 1,000 larvae of the spindle ermine moth species (*Yponomeuta cagnagella*), half of which came from the city and half from the countryside. All got to spend their childhood in similar lighting conditions in a laboratory. Right after hatching, as night fell, they were let out into a large net cage, with a light source placed on the opposite side. Then it was just a matter of waiting the whole night through.

Would city moths and country moths be equally attracted to the light?

The result was clear: city moths were evidently much

less attracted to light, by an average of as much as 30 per cent. This indicates that nocturnal moths that have spent generation after generation living in an artificially lit environment have undergone an evolutionary adaptation to artificial light. After all, it doesn't make much sense for masses of them to fly round and round streetlamps, getting burnt or eaten up by predators that have worked out where the buffet is being served. This could explain the emergence of selective pressure against attraction to light among urban moths.

On the one hand, this is fine, because it prevents them from dying like that. On the other, it can have far-reaching adverse consequences. Because there is a cost attached: the avoidance of light probably means that urban moths simply spend more time sitting still.

Consequently, the effect of artificial light in built-up areas alters the insects' role in the ecosystem. For example, it is difficult for nocturnal insect-eaters to catch an insect that is hidden and motionless. Nor is an insect that can't be bothered to fly going to get much pollination done among flowers adapted to nocturnally active pollinators. That is why it is important to restrict light pollution and, in particular, to try and keep artificial light away from natural areas not yet affected by it.

Warmer, Wetter, Wilder – What About the Beetles?

We know that we are heading towards a future in which the climate will be different. This will also affect insects, both directly and indirectly.

One challenge is that climate changes disturb the finely tuned synchronisations between different species. We see a shift in the timing of many processes, such as the return of migratory birds, and foliation, or spring blossoming. The challenge is that different events do not necessarily shift in sync. If the insect-eating birds produce their young too late or too early in relation to the period when there are most insects, there may be too little food for the chicks in the nest. This can happen if some events are triggered by day length (which is not affected by global warming), while others are triggered by mean temperature, for instance. In the same way, plants that are reliant on particular insects for pollination may suffer poor seed production if they flower at a point when these insects are no longer swarming.

The spring can be particularly challenging, especially 'false springs', which arrive far too early. When that happens, overwintering adult insects are tempted out by the warmth and go in search of food. When the frost returns, the insects will struggle to cope with the cold and with finding enough food because they have poor cold tolerance and few food reserves in the spring.

We see that many insects try to adapt in response to changes in the climate. Sometimes their entire distribution is shifted, but we often see that the species fail to keep up and the distribution shrinks instead. In the case of dragonflies and butterflies, it has been proven that many species have become less widespread and are shifting northwards. Colour charts of the different dragonfly species show that many butterflies and dragonflies, especially those with dark colouring, have vanished from southern Europe and sought refuge in the Northeast, where the climate is cooler. Forecasts produced for bumblebees indicate that we may risk losing between a tenth and – in a worst-case scenario – half of our 69 European varieties by 2100 owing to climate change.

In the North, climate change is increasing the distribution of leaf-eating caterpillars. This also exacerbates the effects on the birch forests, which are being chewed bare. Over the course of a decade, outbreaks of autumnal moths and their relatives have caused considerable damage to the birch forests of Finnmark in northern Norway. The outbreaks have ripple effects on the entire system: food conditions, vegetation and animal life are all changed.

Along with researchers in Tromsø and at the Norwegian University of Life Sciences, I have looked at how the autumnal moths' depredations affect a different group of insects: the beetles that break down the dead birches, thereby ensuring that the nutrients are recycled. Our results show that the attack of the autumnal moths creates so many dead birch trees in such a short space of time that the wood-living beetles are simply unable to keep pace. They cannot respond to the increase in available food with an equivalent increase in the number of individuals. We do not know what effect this may have over the long term, and this illustrates a key point: we have no idea what sort of consequences continued temperature increases will have for the ecosystem in the North, but it is obvious that there will be dramatic changes.

Since one of my research fields is insects in large, ancient and hollow oak trees, I have been wondering how climate change will affect the beetles inhabiting them. A couple of years ago, my research group and some Swedish scientists compared a large dataset that covered beetle communities associated with oak trees across the whole of southern Sweden and southern Norway. The oaks stood in places with differing climates, so that the range they spanned in terms of temperature and precipitation was roughly equivalent to the changes foreseen in climate scenarios. We used this to look at differences in the beetle communities in order to gain knowledge about how a warmer, wetter and wilder climate might affect these different insect communities in the future.

In our study, we found that warmer climates were good for the most specialised and peculiar species. Unfortunately, though, these unique species also reacted badly to increased precipitation. This means that climate change is hardly going to improve conditions for these particular insects. However, the more common species showed few reactions to climate in our study.

This confirms a pattern that is common in our times, not just in relation to climate changes but quite generally: locally unique, specially adapted species are the ones that suffer, whereas common species do fine. This means that many rare and unique species will go into decline, whereas relatively few species that are already common will become commoner still. This is known as ecological homogenisation: the same species are found everywhere and nature becomes more similar across different geographies.

Insecticides and Genetic Manipulation: Dare We, Should We?

Every year, we use massive amounts of chemicals quite intentionally, precisely in order to kill insects. After all, that's the whole point of insecticides used in agriculture, and private homes and gardens.

Many people think the intensive use of pesticides in agriculture is a price we must pay to be able to feed a constantly increasing population through industrial agriculture. Others will argue we ought to take a more ecological approach and cooperate with nature in our agriculture practices, even if this might lead to lower crop yields.

Although we don't have space to go into this discussion here, I must mention the large and growing documentation detailing the unwanted harmful effects of neonicotinoids, a widely used group of insecticides. These substances affect the navigation and immune defences of honeybees and wild bees, and may be among the reasons for the decline in these groups.

We humans have recently acquired a brand-new tool in our battle against insects that are harmful to us. I'm thinking of genetic manipulation, in particular what is somewhat cryptically known as the CRISPR/Cas9 Method. This is like a pair of molecular scissors that can cut up genes and may be used to alter an organism's DNA by removing or exchanging certain genes. The method may be combined with something called a gene driver, which ensures that the genetic change rapidly spreads to pretty much all offspring.

Malaria is caused by a tiny parasite that the mosquito carries with it from one infected person to another when it sucks their blood. Every year, around half a million people die of malaria, most of whom are under five years of age. Even so, the numbers are much lower than they were just 15 years ago, and much of this decrease is down to simple measures, such as the use of insect nets impregnated with insecticide. But now we also have a tool that could ultimately be used to wipe out the malaria mosquito once and for all. This can be achieved by making one of the sexes sterile or by ensuring that all the offspring are the same sex.

This has prompted a timely question from the Norwegian Biotechnology Advisory Board in several different forums: dare we – and should we – use such tools in the natural world? We know little about the impact. One issue is that we don't know what cascading effects this could have in the ecosystem. What if we eliminate one species and another simply steps in and takes over as a spreader of disease? For all we know, things could end up worse than they were to start off with.

Another question is whether the use of a tool like this could lead to undesirable mutations, with undreamt-of consequences. Terrifying scenarios, such as the spread of sterility to other organisms, lie in wait. Despite the need for haste, we must proceed with caution: before we start to use the new gene technology tools to genetically alter or wipe out insects that spread serious diseases we must protect ourselves as best we can against undesirable consequences.

The End of the Giant Bumblebees

We humans have changed a lot of things on this planet. Some are things we cannot change – like the fact that our forefathers already wiped out most of the really big animals, tens of thousands of years ago on continent after continent. Gone were the mammoth, the sabre-tooth tiger and the giant sloth. And along with them, a great many insects almost certainly died out too, insects associated with this megafauna in various ways, although we know even less about them.

Other changes are much more recent. Seagoing explorers brought cats, rats and other efficient predatory mammals to islands where life had gone its own way. Native species that hadn't the wit to look after themselves, species developed in the absence of such enemies, were then often summarily dispatched.

We continue to displace species at a rapid pace, sometimes without meaning to, and sometimes quite intentionally. Like the import of buff-tailed bumblebees to South America, where they were supposed to improve pollination in fruit orchards and greenhouses. The buff-tailed bumblebee has spread rapidly and is crowding out the local giant bumblebee, *Bombus dahlbomii*, apparently because the buff-tailed bumblebee carries parasites that the giant bumblebee can't cope with. The *Bombus dahlbomii* is the world's biggest bumblebee, affectionately described by bumblebee expert Dave Goulson as 'a monstrous fluffy ginger beast'. Soon it might be gone forever.

So, what are we to do with introduced species that threaten unique native species? These are big, difficult and important questions that we need to debate more in society. In some cases, the decision forces itself upon us, as in New Zealand. The government there has launched a plan to wipe out rats, opossums and stoats. These alien species kill roughly 25 million birds every year.

Many other island nations suffer from the same problem. This challenge can be illustrated by a tale from Australia about a once-extinct stick insect that was rediscovered, and the living, but soon-to-be dead black rats that ate it up.

Routing the Rats

On 15 June 1918 the steamship SS *Makambo*, packed to the gunwales with fruit and vegetables, ran aground just off Lord Howe Island, a tropical island far out in the Pacific Ocean. An easterly outpost of Australia, its few inhabitants were separated from the mainland by more than 600 kilometres. The important point about this shipwreck is the rats who managed to reach dry land. In the nine days it took to repair the ship, an unknown number of black rats managed to reach the shore and establish a foothold on the island.

For millions of years Lord Howe Island had lain isolated in the middle of the ocean. Unique species had developed there, species that existed nowhere else on Earth. But the rats hadn't come to chill on the beach. Remember the story of the very hungry caterpillar (*page 6*)? The one that ate its way through an apple on Monday, two pears on Tuesday and ended up ploughing its way through oranges, sausages, ice-cream and chocolate cake before the weekend was over? That's roughly what the rats did on Lord Howe, too, the only difference being that they ate up unique species, one by one. In the early years alone, they finished off at least five species of birds and thirteen small animals that couldn't be found anywhere else in the world.

One of these small creatures was a gigantic stick insect. You know, those thin pale-brown insects that look like dried twigs. But this species wasn't just any old stick insect. We're talking about a quite special insect, the world's heaviest stick insect: it was the size of a big barbecue sausage, dark, shiny and wingless, and aptly went by the nickname of 'tree lobster'. Its Latin name, should you wish to know it, was *Dryococelus australis*. This insect proved to be a slap-up meal for hungry rats. By as early as 1920 the species was already declared extinct – a kind of belated victim of the shipwreck two years earlier.

But this story takes an unexpected turn. Because the outpost has an outpost: 20 kilometres away from Lord Howe Island lies Ball's Pyramid, a sheer narrow sea stack almost twice the height of The Shard in London. For years, it attracted adventurous climbers, but since being awarded World Heritage status in 1982 (along with Lord Howe Island), only scientific expeditions have been allowed to visit. Around this time persistent rumours also began to circulate that there were 'tree lobsters' on the sea stack. And suddenly there was no end to the number of climbing expeditions with an inordinate interest in bugs that were applying for climbing permits to go looking for this rare stick insect. In the end, the man in charge got so sick of assessing climbing permits disguised as insect research that he decided to put an end to the rumours once and for all.

And so, in 2001, two scientists and two assistants travelled to the sea stack. They climbed up the sheer rock face without seeing a single tree lobster, but on their way down, they discovered a small bush of the type eaten by the insect, wedged into a crevice in the rock face. Below lay some large droppings, which looked fresh. Hard as they searched, not a single living stick was to be seen so there was only one thing left to do: repeat the climbing expedition at night – because the world's largest stick insect is known to be nocturnal. Equipped with head-lamps and cameras, the climbers experienced something akin to a waking dream. Unbelievably, there, in the middle of what was pretty much the sole bush on the entire stack, sat 24 huge black stick insects, staring at them.

Nobody can say how the insects made their way from Lord Howe Island to the sea stack some time before the extinction in 1920. If you can't fly or swim, a 20-kilometre trip across the open sea is quite a challenge. The most likely explanation is that eggs or a pregnant female hitched a ride with a bird or on floating vegetation and then managed to survive for at least 80 years on the inhospitable sea stack that is almost entirely bare of vegetation.

We will draw a veil of silence over the bureaucracy that ensued. After two years of paper-shuffling, permission was finally obtained for two males and two females to be fetched from the sea stack to form the start of a breed-ing programme. Two of them (christened Adam and Eve, of course) survived by the skin of their teeth and healthy stocks of stick insects can now be found in several zoos, including Europe. But then the question arose of returning the rest of them to Lord Howe Island, where the species actually belonged. Because a sea stack with a single bush at the mercy of rock falls is hardly fit to be a permanent home for a viable population of stick insects living in the wild. But on Lord Howe, the black rats still prevail. Unless they are wiped out, there's no point reintroducing the stick insects. And they aren't the only creatures who would be glad to see the rats killed off: 13 bird species and two reptile species face extinction unless the rats are eliminated so the authorities now plan to do away with the rats once and for all. This requires extreme measures: 42 tonnes of poisoned cereal will be scattered over the island from a helicopter.

Of course, it isn't entirely straightforward. First of all, animals other than the rats may die from eating the grain – including the birds that people are trying to rescue. So, the idea is to trap the most vulnerable bird species and keep them in a kind of temporary Noah's Ark, then release them again after the poison rain. But what consequences will this have for the genetic diversity of the birds, for example – because it won't be possible to capture all the individuals, will it?

And then some people are worried. There are only 350 human inhabitants on the island but not all of them are keen on being showered with poisoned breakfast cereal, even though the authorities have assured them that no poison will be scattered near houses. Some probably also think that the big black stick insects are repulsive and no more deserving of protection than the black rats. Because conservation biology is just as much about us humans and our thoughts and feelings as about the species we are trying to conserve.

New Times, New Species

In many ways, nature is robust and it is adapting all the time. New species emerge where we humans create new opportunities. Like deep below the ground in London, where the rough damp tunnels of the Tube are home to a highly unusual mosquito. It belongs to the *Culex pipiens* species, the most common type of blood-sucking mosquito found in urban areas, but has developed into a special genetic form (called *molestus* – 'the troublesome one'), which is no longer capable of producing offspring with its mosquito relatives up in the light of day. What almost certainly happened is that a couple of female mosquitoes found their way down into the depths at some point many years ago, perhaps when the Tube was being built in 1863. And since then, the London Underground mosquito has lived its own life down there, over hundreds of mosquito generations.

The mosquito became notorious during the Second World War when it was a source of great irritation to people seeking shelter in the Underground system during the Blitz. Today, standards are far better than in those days and although roe deer, foxes, bats, woodpeckers, sparrow hawks, tortoises and great crested newts have all been spotted in the tunnels, rats and mice are the main species that keep the few London Underground mosquitoes company.

Genetic analyses have shown that the mosquitoes' DNA varies between lines and stations: the Piccadilly Line mosquito is different from the Central Line mosquito – although not different enough to prevent the various Underground mosquitoes from mating with one another. The leading theory is therefore that all of them are descendants of the same bold forebears from 150 years ago.

If it is true that the mosquito has developed into a new genetic form in just 150 years, this is an example of how evolution can work quickly now and then – as when populations are living in total isolation. Charles Darwin envisaged that new species needed tens of thousands, if not hundreds of thousands of generations to come into being. It is odd to think that while he sat pondering this in his house on the outskirts of London – he had just published *On the Origin of Species* in 1859 – a process of lightning-fast evolution may perhaps have been starting beneath his feet.

We will probably see more such examples of new and rapid species formation in the future as a result of our intentional and unintentional displacement of species. The North American fly, *Rhagoletis pomonella*, used to live contentedly on hawthorn trees until apples came to the US from Europe. Now the fly has two different genetic forms

– one that only eats hawthorn berries and another that only eats apples. In just a couple of hundred years, one species is well on its way to becoming two. Even the parasite that lives on this fly is in the process of splitting into two species, one for the hawthorn-eating and one for the apple-eating larva.

When new insects appear and others die out, the effect will depend on which species change. Because, as I have shown in this book, different insects perform different tasks in nature. What's more, every single insect is connected to other species through ingeniously adapted interactions, and this is the basis for all the goods and services nature offers us.

We humans have long taken the free services of insects for granted. Through intensive land use, climate change, insecticides and invasive species, we now risk altering conditions so quickly that insects will have difficulty delivering as they have done to date, despite nature's adaptability. On egotistical grounds alone, we should therefore be concerned about the health and wellbeing of these little critters. Taking care of them is a form of life insurance for our children and grandchildren.

If we could only stop navel-gazing for a second, we would see that this is about more than mere utility value.

As far as we know, our planet is the only place in the universe where there is life. Many would say that we humans have a moral duty to rein in our dominance of the Earth and give our millions of fellow creatures a chance to live out their tiny, wonderful lives too.

Afterword

Somewhere far back in the mists of time we share a common forebear with the insects. Although insects arrived long before us – they have a headstart of several hundred million years – we also have a long, shared history, for better and for worse. And there is no doubt that we need them. As the Harvard professor E. O. Wilson writes: 'The truth is that we need invertebrates but they don't need us. If human beings were to disappear tomorrow, the world would go on with little change. (...) But if invertebrates were to disappear, I doubt that the human species could live more than a few months.'

This means we have everything to gain by caring a bit more about insects. I believe in knowledge, positive talk and enthusiasm. Be curious about bugs, take the time to look and learn. Teach children about all the strange and useful things insects do. Talk nicely about bugs. Make your garden a better place for flower visitors. Let's get insects on the agenda in land-use plans and official reports, in agricultural regulations and state budgets. Let us take pleasure in colourful butterflies, let us admire the funny interactions between these little critters and be thankful that insects step up to work on our behalf.

Insects are strange, intricate, funny, bizarre, fun, charming, unique and never cease to amaze us. A Canadian entomologist once said: 'The world is rich in small wonders – but so poor in eyes that see them.' My hope is that this book will open more people's eyes to the weird and wonderful world of insects – and the extraordinary little lives they live alongside us on this planet we share.

Thanks

I've had loads of great discussions about insects and related matters over the years. Thanks to my fantastic colleague Tone Birkemoe, at NMBU, for her unwavering enthusiasm, productive conversations and comments on this text. And three cheers for all the other members of the NBMU's insect group, who all help talk up insects and make it a fun working environment. Thanks to my former colleagues at NINA (where I still have the pleasure of working part-time) – and to former Head of Research Erik Framstad as a representative for everybody there – for all the stimulating conversations about absolutely everything between heaven and earth.

Thanks to my family, close and extended alike. My parents taught me to be curious about everything that moved outdoors in nature. I believe my mother has read, heard, watched and said something nice about every single communicative idea I've been involved with over the past few years. Thanks to my dear Kjetil for all the patience, tea, and buttered crispbread he has served up during late nights of writing. Thanks to our children, Simen, Tuva and Karine, for all the fun we have together, and a special thank-you to Tuva for casting a sharp eye over the text and for drawing the chapter illustrations.

Thanks to Lucy Moffatt for doing a brilliant job on the English translation, to Carim Nahaboo for creating the wonderful full-page illustrations, and to my editor, Lydia Good, for her excellent and enthusiastic work.

Last, but not least, it has been incredible fun writing this book. I've taken such joy in everything I've learnt. And my publishers have been with me all the way. Thanks for that, and thanks for the support I received from the Norwegian Non-Fiction Writers and Translators Association's Non-Fiction Literature Fund.

Further Reading

These books have brought me great pleasure and inspiration, both generally and while writing this book. I recommend them to any readers keen to take a deeper dive into the fantastic world of the insects:

Berenbaum, M. B. *Bugs in the System*, Addison-Wesley, Reading, Massachusetts, 1995.

The books of Dave Goulson: *A Sting in the Tale* (2013), *A Buzz in the Meadow* (2014) and *Bee Quest* (2017), all published by Jonathan Cape, London.

Jones, R. *Call of Nature: The Secret Life of Dung*, Pelagic Publishing, Exeter, UK, 2017.

McAlister, E. *The Secret Life of Flies*, Natural History Museum, London, 2017.

Shaw, S. R. *Planet of the Bugs: Evolution and the Rise of Insects*, University of Chicago Press, Chicago, 2014.

Zuk, M. *Sex on Six Legs: Lessons on Life, Love, and Language from the Insect World,* Houghton Mifflin Harcourt, 2011.

Sources

Introduction

Andersen, T., Baranov, V., Hagenlund, L.K. et al. 'Blind Flight? A New Troglobiotic Orthoclad (Diptera, Chironomidae) from the Lukina Jama – Trojama Cave in Croatia', PLOS ONE 11 (2016), e0152884.

Artsdatabanken. 'Hvor mange arter finnes i Norge?' sourced in 2017 from https://www.artsdatabanken.no/Pages/205713.

Baust, J. G. & Lee, R. E. 'Multiple Stress Tolerance in an Antarctic Terrestrial Arthropod: *Belgica antarctica*', *Cryobiology* 24 (1987), pp. 140–7.

Berenbaum, M. B. *Bugs in the System*, Addison-Wesley, Reading, Massachusetts, 1995.

Bishopp, F. C. 'Domestic Mosquitoes', US Department of Agriculture, Leaflet No. 186 (1939).

Fang, J. 'Ecology: A World Without Mosquitoes', *Nature* 466 (2010), pp. 432–4.

Guinness World Records. 'Largest Species of beetle', from http://www.guinnessworldrecords.com/world-records/largest-species-of-beetle/ (2017).

Huber, J. T. & Noyes, J. 'A New Genus and Species of Fairyfly, *Tinkerbella nana* (Hymenoptera, Mymaridae), with

Comments on its Sister Genus *Kikiki*, and Discussion on Small Size Limits in Arthropods', *Journal of Hymenoptera Research* 32 (2013), pp. 17–44.

Kadavy, D. R., Myatt, J., Plantz, B. A. et al. 'Microbiology of the Oil Fly, *Helaeomyia petrolei*', *Applied and Environmental Microbiology* 65 (1999), pp. 1477–82.

Kelley, J. L., Peyton, J. T., Fiston-Lavier, A.-S. et al. 'Compact Genome of the Antarctic Midge Is Likely an Adaptation to an Extreme Environment', *Nature Communications* 5 (2014), Article No. 4611.

Knapp, F. W. 'Arthropod Pests of Horses', in Williams, R. E., Hall, R. D., Broce, A. B. & Scholl, P. J. (Eds): *Livestock Entomology*. Wiley, New York (1985), pp. 297–322.

Leonardi, M. & Palma, R. 'Review of the Systematics, Biology and Ecology of Lice from Pinnipeds and River Otters (Insecta: Phthiraptera: Anoplura: Echinophthiriidae)'. *Zootaxa*, 3630(3) (2013), pp. 445–66.

Misof, B., Liu, S., Meusemann, K. et al. 'Phylogenomics Resolves the Timing and Pattern of Insect Evolution'. *Science* 346 (2014), pp. 763–7.

Nesbitt, S. J., Barrett, P. M., Werning, S. et al. 'The Oldest Dinosaur? A Middle Triassic Dinosauriform from Tanzania', *Biology Letters* 9 (2013).

Shaw, S. R. *Planet of the Bugs. Evolution and the Rise of Insects*. University of Chicago Press, Chicago (2014).

Xinhuanet. 'World's Longest Insect Discovered in China', sourced in 2017 from http://news.xinhuanet.com/english/2016-05/05/c_135336786.htm (2016).

Zuk, M. *Sex on Six Legs: Lessons on Life, Love, and Language from the Insect World*, Houghton Mifflin Harcourt, 2011.

CHAPTER 1:
Small Creatures, Smart Design: Insect Anatomy

Alem, S., Perry, C. J., Zhu, X. et al. 'Associative Mechanisms Allow for Social Learning and Cultural Transmission of String Pulling in an Insect', *PLOS Biology* 14 (2016), e1002564.

Arikawa, K. 'Hindsight of Butterflies', *BioScience* 51 (2001), pp. 219–25.

Arikawa, K., Eguchi, E., Yoshida, A. & Aoki, K. 'Multiple Extraocular Photoreceptive Areas on Genitalia of Butterfly *Papilio xuthus*', *Nature* 288 (1980), pp. 700–2.

Avarguès-Weber, A., Portelli, G., Benard, J. et al. 'Configural Processing Enables Discrimination and Categorization of Face-Like Stimuli in Honeybees', *The Journal of Experimental Biology* 213 (2010), pp. 593–601.

Caro, T. M. & Hauser, M. D. 'Is There Teaching in Nonhuman Animals?' *The Quarterly Review of Biology* 67 (1992), pp. 151–74.

Chapman, A. D. *Numbers of Living Species in Australia and the World* (2nd ed.), Canberra, 2009.

Dacke, M. & Srinivasan, M. V. 'Evidence for Counting in Insects', *Animal Cognition* 11 (2008), pp. 683–9.

Darwin, C. *Charles Darwin's Beagle Diary* (1834), sourced in 2017 from http://darwinbeagle.blogspot.no/2009/09/17th-september-1834.html

Darwin, C. *The Descent of Man, and Selection in Relation to Sex*. J. Murray, London, 1871.

Elven, H. & Aarvik, L. 'Insekter Insecta', sourced in 2017 from Artsdatabanken https://artsdatabanken.no/Pages/135656 (2017).

Falck, M. 'La vevkjerringene veve videre', *Insektnytt* 29 (2004), pp. 57–60.

Franks, N. R. & Richardson, T. 'Teaching in Tandem-Running Ants', *Nature* 439 (2006), p. 153.

Frye, M. A. 'Visual Attention: A Cell that Focuses on One Object at a Time'. Current Biology 23 (2013), R61–3.

Gonzalez-Bellido, P. T., Peng, H., Yang, J. et al. 'Eight Pairs of Descending Visual Neurons in the Dragonfly Give Wing Motor Centers Accurate Population Vector of Prey Direction', *Proceedings of the National Academy of Sciences* 110 (2013), pp. 696–701.

Gopfert, M. C., Surlykke, A. & Wasserthal, L. T. 'Tympanal and Atympanal "Mouth-Ears" in Hawkmoths (Sphingidae)'. *Proc Biol Sci* 269 (2002), pp. 89–95.

Jabr, F. 'How Did Insect Metamorphosis Evolve?' Sourced in 2017 from https://www.scienti camerican.com/article/insect-metamorphosis-evolution/ (2012).

Leadbeater, E. & Chittka, L. 'Social Learning in Insects – From Miniature Brains to Consensus Building', *Current Biology* 17 (2007), R703–R713.

Minnich, D. E. 'The Chemical Sensitivity of the Legs of the Blowfly, *Calliphora vomitoria* Linn., to Various Sugars', *Zeitschrift für vergleichende Physiologie* 11 (1929), pp. 1–55.

Montealegre-Z., F., Jonsson, T., Robson-Brown, K. A. et al. 'Convergent Evolution Between Insect and Mammalian Audition', *Science* 338 (2012), pp. 968–71.

Munz, T. *The Dancing Bees: Karl von Frisch and the Discovery of the Honeybee Language*, The University of Chicago, 2016.

'Eremitten yttes til åpen soning'. Press. NINA. Sourced in 2017 from http://www.nina.no/english/News/News-article/ArticleId/4321 (2017).

Ranius, T. & Hedin, J. 'The Dispersal Rate of a Beetle, *Osmoderma eremita*, Living in Tree Hollows', *Oecologia* 126 (2001), pp. 363–70.

Shuker, K. P. N. *The Hidden Powers of Animals: Uncovering the Secrets of Nature*, Marshall Editions Ltd., London, 2001.

Tibbetts, E. A. 'Visual Signals of Individual Identity in the Wasp *Polistes fuscatus*', *Proceedings of the Royal Society of London. Series B: Biological Sciences* 269 (2002), pp. 1423–8.

CHAPTER 2:
Six-legged Sex: Dating, Mating and Parenting

Banerjee, S., Coussens, N. P., Gallat, F. X. et al. 'Structure of a Heterogeneous, Glycosylated, Lipid-Bound, in Vivo-Grown Protein Crystal at Atomic Resolution from the Viviparous Cockroach *Diploptera punctate*', *IUCrJ* 3 (2016), pp. 282–93.

Birch, J. & Okasha, S. 'Kin Selection and Its Critics', *BioScience* 65 (2015), pp. 22–32.

Boos, S., Meunier, J., Pichon, S. & Kölliker, M. 'Maternal Care Provides Antifungal Protection to Eggs in the European Earwig', *Behavioral Ecology* 25 (2014), pp. 754–61.

Borror, D. J., Triplehorn, C. A. & Johnson, N. F. *An Introduction to the Study of Insects*, Saunders College Pub, Philadelphia, 1989.

Brian, M. B. *Production Ecology of Ants and Termites*, Cambridge University Press, 1978.

Eady, P. E. & Brown, D. V. 'Male-female Interactions Drive the (Un)repeatability of Copula Duration in an Insect', *Royal Society Open Science* 4 (2017), 160962.

Eberhard, W. G. 'Copulatory Courtship and Cryptic Female Choice in Insects', *Biological Reviews* 66 (1991), pp. 1–31.

Fedina, T. Y. 'Cryptic Female Choice during Spermatophore Transfer in *Tribolium castaneum* (Coleoptera: Tenebrionidae)', *Journal of Insect Physiology* 53 (2007), pp. 93–98.

Fleming, N. 'Which Life Form Dominates on Earth?' Sourced in 2017 from http://www.bbc.com/earth/story/20150211-whats-the-most-dominant-life-form (2015).

Folkehelseinstituttet. 'Hjortelusflue', sourced in 2017 from https://www.fhi.no/nettpub/skadedyrveilederen/fluer-og-mygg/hjortelusflue-/ (2015).

Hamill, J. 'What a Buzz Kill: Male Bees' Testicles EXPLODE When They Reach Orgasm', sourced in 2017 from https://www.thesun.co.uk/news/1926328/male-bees-testicles-explode-when-they-reach-orgasm/ (2016)

Lawrence, S. E. 'Sexual Cannibalism in the Praying Mantid, *Mantis religiosa*: A Field Study', *Animal Behaviour* 43 (1992), pp. 569–83.

Lüpold, S., Manier, M. K., Puniamoorthy, N. et al. 'How Sexual Selection Can Drive the Evolution of Costly Sperm Ornamentation', *Nature* (2016), pp. 533–5.

Maderspacher, F. 'All the Queen's Men', *Current Biology* 17 (2007), R191–R195.

Nowak, M. A., Tarnita, C. E. & Wilson, E. O. 'The Evolution of Eusociality', *Nature* 466 (2010), pp. 1057–62.

Pitnick, S., Spicer, G. S. & Markow, T. A. 'How Long Is a Giant Sperm?' *Nature* 375 (1995), p. 109.

Schwartz, S. K., Wagner, W. E. & Hebets, E. A. 'Spontaneous Male Death and Monogyny in the Dark Fishing Spider', *Biology Letters* 9 (2013).

Shepard, M., Waddil, V. & Kloft, W. 'Biology of the Predaceous

Earwig *Labidura riparia* (Dermaptera: Labiduridae)', *Annals of the Entomological Society of America* 66 (1973), pp. 837–41.

Sivinski, J. 'Intrasexual Aggression in the Stick Insects *Diapheromera veliei* and *D. Covilleae* and Sexual Dimorphism in the Phasmatodea', *Psyche* 85 (1978), pp. 395–405.

Williford, A., Stay, B. & Bhattacharya, D. 'Evolution of a Novel Function: Nutritive Milk in the Viviparous Cockroach, *Diploptera punctate*', *Evolution & Development* 6 (2004), pp. 67–77.

CHAPTER 3:
Eat or Be Eaten: Insects in the Food Chain

Britten, K. H., Thatcher, T. D. & Caro, T. 'Zebras and Biting Flies: Quantitative Analysis of Reflected Light from Zebra Coats in Their Natural Habitat', *PLOS ONE* 11 (2016), e0154504.

Caro, T., Izzo, A., Reiner Jr., R. C. et al. 'The Function of Zebra Stripes', *Nature Communications* 5 (2014), 3535.

Caro, T. & Stankowich, T. 'Concordance on Zebra Stripes: A Comment on Larison et al. *Royal Society Open Science* 2 (2015).

Darwin, C. Darwin Correspondence Project. Sourced in 2017 from http://www.darwinproject.ac.uk/letter/DCP-LETT-2814.xml (1860).

Dheilly, N. M., Maure, F., Ravallec, M. et al. 'Who Is the Puppet Master? Replication of a Parasitic Wasp-Associated Virus Correlates with Host Behaviour Manipulation', *Proceedings of the Royal Society B: Biological Sciences* 282 (2015).

Eberhard, W. G. 'The Natural History and Behavior of the

Bolas Spider *Mastophora dizzydeani* SP. n. (Araneidae)', *Psyche* 87 (1980), pp. 143–169.

Haynes, K. F., Gemeno, C., Yeargan, K. V. et al. 'Aggressive Chemical Mimicry of Moth Pheromones by a Bolas Spider: How Does This Specialist Predator Attract More Than One Species of Prey?', *Chemoecology* 12 (2002), pp. 99–105.

Larison, B., Harrigan, R. J., Thomassen, H. A. et al. 'How the Zebra Got its Stripes: A Problem with Too Many Solutions', *Royal Society Open Science* 2 (2015).

Libersat, F. & Gal, R. 'What Can Parasitoid Wasps Teach us about Decision-Making in Insects?' *Journal of Experimental Biology* 216 (2013), pp. 47–55.

Marshall, D. C. & Hill, K. B. R. 'Versatile Aggressive Mimicry of Cicadas by an Australian Predatory Katydid', *PLOS ONE* 4 (2009), e4185.

Melin, A. D., Kline, D. W., Hiramatsu, C. & Caro, T. 'Zebra Stripes Through the Eyes of their Predators, Zebras, and Humans', PLOS ONE 11(2016), e0145679.

Yeargan, K. V. 'Biology of Bolas Spiders', *Annual Review of Entomology* 39 (1994), pp. 81–99.

CHAPTER 4:
Insects and Plants: A Never-ending Race

Babikova, Z., Gilbert, L., Bruce, T. J. A. et al. 'Underground Signals Carried Through Common Mycelial Networks Warn Neighbouring Plants of Aphid Attack', *Ecology Letters* 16 (2013), pp. 835–43.

Barbero, F., Patricelli, D., Witek, M. et al. 'Myrmica Ants and Their Butterfly Parasites with Special Focus on the Acoustic Communication', *Psyche* 2012: 11 (2012).

Dangles, O. & Casas, J. 'The Bee and the Turtle: A Fable from Yasuní National Park', *Frontiers in Ecology and the Environment* 10 (2012), pp. 446–7.

de la Rosa, C. L. 'Additional Observations of Lachryphagous Butterflies and Bees', *Frontiers in Ecology and the Environment* 12 (2014), p. 210.

Department of Agriculture and Fisheries, B. Q. 'The Prickly Pear Story', sourced in 2017 from https://www.daf.qld.gov.au/__data/assets/pdf_le/0014/55301/IPA-Prickly-Pear-Story-PP62.pdf (2016).

Ekblom, R. 'Smörbolls ugornas fantastiska värld', *Fauna och Flora* 102 (2007) pp. 20–22.

Evans, T. A., Dawes, T. Z., Ward, P. R. & Lo, N. 'Ants and Termites Increase Crop Yield in a Dry Climate', *Nature Communications* 2: (2011), Article No. 262.

Grinath, J. B., Inouye, B. D. & Underwood, N. 'Bears Benefit Plants Via a Cascade with both Antagonistic and Mutualistic Interactions', *Ecology Letters* 18 (2015), pp. 164–73.

Hansen, L. O. *Pollinerende insekter i Maridalen*. Årsskrift. 132 pages, Maridalens Venner, 2015.

Hölldobler, B. & Wilson, E. O. *Journey to the Ants: A Story of Scientific Exploration*, Belknap Press of Harvard University Press, Cambridge, Massachusetts, 1994.

Lengyel, S., Gove, A. D., Latimer, A. M. et al. 'Convergent Evolution of Seed Dispersal by Ants, and Phylogeny and Biogeography in Flowering Plants: A Global Survey', *Perspectives in Plant Ecology Evolution and Systematics* 12 (2010), pp. 43–55.

McAlister, E. *The Secret Life of Flies*. Natural History Museum, London, 2017.

Midgley, J. J., White, J. D. M., Johnson, S. D. & Bronner, G.

N. 'Faecal Mimicry by Seeds Ensures Dispersal by Dung Beetles', *Nature Plants* 1 (2015), 15141.

Moffett, M. W. *Adventures Among Ants. A Global Safari with a Cast of Trillions*, University of California Press, 2010.

Nedham, J. *Science and Civilisation in China. Volume 6, Biology and Biological Technology: Part 1: Botany*, Cambridge University Press, Cambridge, UK, 1986.

Oliver, T. H., Mashanova, A., Leather, S. R. et al. *Ant semiochemicals limit apterous aphid dispersal. Proceedings of the Royal Society B: Biological Sciences* 274 (2007), pp. 3127–31.

Patricelli, D., Barbero, F., Occhipinti, A. et al. 'Plant Defences Against Ants Provide a Pathway to Social Parasitism in Butterflies', *Proceedings of the Royal Society B: Biological Sciences* 282 (2015), 20151111.

Simard, S. W., Perry, D. A., Jones, M. D. et al. 'Net Transfer of Carbon between Ectomycorrhizal Tree Species in the Field', *Nature* 388 (1997), pp. 579–82.

Stiling, P., Moon, D. & Gordon, D. 'Endangered Cactus Restoration: Mitigating the Non-Target Effects of a Biological Control Agent (*Cactoblastis cactorum*) in Florida', *Restoration Ecology* 12 (2004), pp. 605–10.

Stockan, J. A. & Robinson, E. J. H. (Eds). *Wood Ant Ecology and Conservation. Ecology, Biodiversity and Conservation*, Cambridge University Press, Cambridge, 2016.

Wardle, D. A., Hyodo, F., Bardgett, R. D. et al. 'Long-term Aboveground and Belowground Consequences of Red Wood Ant Exclusion in Boreal Forest', *Ecology* 92 (2011), 645–56.

Warren, R. J. & Giladi, I. 'Ant-Mediated Seed Dispersal: A Few Ant Species (Hymenoptera: Formicidae) Benefit many Plants', *Myrmecological News* 20 (2014), pp. 129–40.

Zimmermann, H. G., Moran, V. C. & Hoffmann, J. H. 'The Renowned Cactus Moth, *Cactoblastis cactorum* (Lepidoptera: Pyralidae): Its Natural History and Threat to Native *Opuntia* Floras in Mexico and the United States of America', *Florida Entomologist* 84 (2001) pp. 543–51.

CHAPTER 5:

Busy Flies, Flavoursome Bugs: Insects and Our Food

Bartomeus, I., Potts, S. G., Steffan-Dewenter, I. et al. 'Contribution of Insect Pollinators to Crop Yield and Quality Varies with Agricultural Intensification', *PeerJ* 2 (2014), e328.

Crittenden, A. N. 'The Importance of Honey Consumption in Human Evolution', *Food and Foodways* 19 (2011), pp. 257–73.

Davidson, L. 'Don't Panic, but We Could Be Running Out of Chocolate', sourced in 2017 from http://www.telegraph.co.uk/finance/newsbysector/retailandconsumer/11236558/Dont-panic-but-we-could-be-running-out-of-chocolate.html (2014).

DeLong, D. M. 'Homoptera', sourced in 2017 from https://www.britannica.com/animal/homopteran#ref134267 (2014).

Financial Times, 'Edible Insects: Grub Pioneers Aim to Make Bugs Palatable', sourced in 2018 from https://www.ft.com/content/bc0e4526-ab8d-11e4-b05a-00144feab7de (2015).

Harpaz, I. 'Early Entomology in the Middle East', pp. 21–36 in Smith, R. F., Mittler, T. E. & Smith, C. N. (Eds) *History of Entomology*, Annual Review, Palo Alto, California, (1973).

Hogendoorn, K., Bartholomaeus, F. & Keller, M. A. 'Chemical

and Sensory Comparison of Tomatoes Pollinated by Bees and by a Pollination Wand', *Journal of Economic Entomology* 103 (2010), pp. 1286–92.

Hornetjuice.com. 'About Hornet juice', sourced in 2017 from https:// www.hornetjuice.com/what/

Isack, H. A. & Reyer, H. U. 'Honeyguides and Honey Gatherers: Interspecific Communication in a Symbiotic Relationship', *Science* 243 (1989), pp. 1343–6.

Klatt, B. K., Holzschuh, A., Westphal, C. et al. 'Bee Pollination Improves Crop Quality, Shelf Life and Commercial Value', *Proceedings of the Royal Society B: Biological Sciences* 281 (2014).

Klein, A.-M., Steffan-Dewenter, I. & Tscharntke, T. 'Bee Pollination and Fruit Set of *Coffea arabica* and *C. canephora* (Rubiaceae)', *American Journal of Botany* 90 (2003), pp. 153–7.

Lomsadze, G. 'Report: Georgia Unearths the World's Oldest Honey', sourced in 2017 from http://www.eurasianet.org/ node/65204 (2012).

Ott, J. 'The Delphic Bee: Bees and Toxic Honeys as Pointers to Psychoactive and other Medicinal Plants', *Economic Botany* 52 (1998), pp. 260–66.

Spottiswoode, C. N., Begg, K. S. & Begg, C. M. 'Reciprocal Signaling in Honeyguide-Human Mutualism', *Science* 353 (2016), pp. 387–9.

Språkrådet. 'Språklig insekt i mat', sourced in 2017 from http:// www.sprakradet.no/Vi-og-vart/Publikasjoner/Spraaknytt/ spraknytt-2015/spraknytt-12015/spraklig-insekt-i-mat/ (2015).

Totland, Ø., Hovstad, K. A., Ødegaard, F. & Åström, J. 'Kunnskapsstatus for insektpollinering i Norge – betydningen av det komplekse samspillet mellom planter og insekter', Artsdatabanken, Norge (2013).

Wotton, R. 'What Was Manna?' *Opticon1826* 9 (2010).

CHAPTER 6:
The Circle of Life – and Death: Insects as Caretakers

Barton, D. N., Vågnes Traaholt, N., Blumentrath, S. & Reinvang, R. 'Naturen i Oslo er verdt milliarder. Verdsetting av urbane økosystemtjenester fra grønnstruktur', *NINA Rapport* 1113, 21 pages (2015).

Cambefort, Y. 'Le scarabée dans l'Égypte ancienne. Origine et signification du symbole', *Revue de l'histoire des religions* 204 (1987), pp. 3–46.

Dacke, M., Baird, E., Byrne, M. et al. 'Dung Beetles Use the Milky Way for Orientation', *Current Biology* 23 (2013), pp. 298–300.

Direktoratet for naturforvaltning. 'Handlingsplan for utvalgt naturtype hule eiker', *DN Rapport* 1-2012. 80 pages. (2012).

Eisner, T. & Eisner, M. 'Defensive Use of a Fecal Thatch by a Beetle Larva (*Hemisphaerota cyanea*)', *Proceedings of the National Academy of Sciences of the United States of America* 97 (2000), pp. 2632–6.

Evju, M. (red.), Bakkestuen, V., Blom, H. H., Brandrud, T. E., Bratli, & H. N. B., Sverdrup-Thygeson, A. & Ødegaard, F. 'Oaser for artsmangfoldet – hotspot-habitater for rødlistearter', *NINA Temahefte* 61, 48 pages (2015).

Goff, M. L. *A Fly for the Prosecution: How Insect Evidence Helps Solve Crimes*, Harvard University Press, Cambridge, Mass., 2001.

Gough, L. A., Birkemoe, T. & Sverdrup-Thygeson, A. 'Reactive

Forest Management Can Also Be Proactive for Wood-living Beetles in Hollow Oak Trees', *Biological Conservation* 180 (2014), pp. 75–83.

Jacobsen, R. M. 'Saproxylic insects influence community assembly and succession of fungi in dead wood', PhD thesis, Norwegian University of Life Sciences (2017).

Jacobsen, R. M., Birkemoe, T. & Sverdrup-Thygeson, A. 'Priority Effects of Early Successional Insects Influence Late Successional Fungi in Dead Wood', *Ecology and Evolution* 5 (2015), pp. 4896–4905.

Jones, R. *Call of Nature: The Secret Life of Dung.* Pelagic Publishing, Exeter, UK, 2017.

Ledford, H. 'The Tell-Tale Grasshopper. Can Forensic Science Rely on the Evidence of Bugs?' http://www.nature.com/news/2007/070619/full/news070618-5.html (2007).

McAlister, E. *The Secret Life of Flies*, Natural History Museum, London, 2017.

Parker, C. B. 'Buggy: Entomology Prof Helps Unravel Murder', sourced in 2017 from https://www.ucdavis.edu/news/buggy-entomology-prof-helps-unravel-murder (2007).

Pauli, J. N., Mendoza, J. E., Steffan, S. A. et al. 'A Syndrome of Mutualism Reinforces the Lifestyle of a Sloth', *Proceedings of the Royal Society B: Biological Sciences* 281 (2014).

Pilskog, H. 'Effects of Climate, Historical Logging and Spatial Scales on Beetles in Hollow Oaks', PhD thesis, Norwegian University of Life Sciences (2016).

Savage, A. M., Hackett, B., Guénard, B. et al. 'Fine-Scale Heterogeneity across Manhattan's Urban Habitat Mosaic Is Associated with Variation in Ant Composition and Richness', *Insect Conservation and Diversity* 8 (2015), pp. 216–28.

Storaunet, K. O. & Rolstad, J. 'Mengde og utvikling av død ved produktiv skog i Norge. Med basis i data fra Landsskogtak-seringens 7. (1994–1998) og 10. takst (2010–13). *Oppdrag-srapport* 06/2015, Norsk institutt for skog og landskap, Ås (2015).

Strong, L. 'Avermectins – a Review of their Impact on Insects of Cattle Dung', *Bulletin of Entomological Research,* 82 (1992), pp. 265–74.

Suutari, M., Majaneva, M., Fewer, D. P. et al. 'Molecular Evidence for a Diverse Green Algal Community Growing in the Hair of Sloths and a Specific Association with *Trichophilus welckeri* (Chlorophyta, Ulvophyceae)', *BMC Evolutionary Biology* 10 (2010), p. 86.

Sverdrup-Thygeson, A., Brandrud T. E. (red.), Bratli, H. et al. 'Hotspots – naturtyper med mange truete arter. En gjennomgang av Rødlista for arter 2010 i forbindelse med ARKO-prosjektet', *NINA Rapport* 683, 64 pages (2011).

Sverdrup-Thygeson, A., Skarpaas, O., Blumentrath, S. et al. 'Habitat Connectivity Affects Specialist Species Richness More Than Generalists in Veteran Trees', *Forest Ecology and Management* 403 (2017), pp. 96–102.

Sverdrup-Thygeson, A., Skarpaas, O. & Odegaard, F. 'Hollow Oaks and Beetle Conservation: the Significance of the Surroundings', *Biodiversity and Conservation* 19 (2010), pp. 837–52.

Vencl, F. V., Trillo, P. A. & Geeta, R. 'Functional Interactions Among Tortoise Beetle Larval Defenses Reveal Trait Suites and Escalation', *Behavioral Ecology and Sociobiology* 65 (2011), pp. 227–39.

Wall, R. & Beynon, S. 'Area-wide Impact of Macrocyclic Lac-tone Parasiticides in Cattle Dung', *Medical and Veterinary Entomology* 26 (2012), pp. 1–8.

Welz, A. 'Bird-killing Vet Drug Alarms European Conservationists', sourced in 2017 from https://www.theguardian.com/environment/nature-up/2014/mar/11/bird-killing-vet-drug-alarms-european-conservationists (2014).

Youngsteadt, E., Henderson, R. C., Savage, A. M. et al. 'Habitat and Species Identity, not Diversity, Predict the Extent of Refuse Consumption by Urban Arthropods', *Global Change Biology* 21 (2015), pp. 1103–15.

Ødegaard, F., Hansen, L. O. & Sverdrup-Thygeson, A. 'Dyremøkk – et hotspot-habitat. Sluttrapport under ARKO-prosjektets periode II', *NINA Rapport* 715, 42 pages, (2011).

Ødegaard, F., Sverdrup-Thygeson, A., Hansen, L. O. et al. 'Kartlegging av invertebrater i fem hotspot-habitattyper. Nye norske arter og rødlistearter 2004–2008', *NINA Rapport* 500, 102 pages (2009).

CHAPTER 7:

From Silk to Shellac: Industries of Insects

Andersson, M., Jia, Q., Abella, A. et al. 'Biomimetic Spinning of Artificial Spider Silk from a Chimeric Minispidroin', *Nature Chemical Biology* 13 (2017) pp. 262–4.

Apéritif.no. 'De nødvendige tanninene', sourced in 2017 from https://www.aperitif.no/artikler/de-nodvendige-tanninene/169203 (2014).

Bower, C. F. 'Mind Your Beeswax', sourced in 2017 from https://www.catholic.com/magazine/print-edition/mind-your-beeswax (1991).

Copeland, C. G., Bell, B. E., Christensen, C. D. & Lewis, R. V. 'Development of a Process for the Spinning of Synthetic

Spider Silk', *ACS Biomaterials Science & Engineering* 1 (2015), pp. 577–84.

Europalov.no. 'Tilsetningsforordningen: endringsbestemmelser om bruk av stoffer på eggeskall', sourced in 2017 from http://europalov.no/rettsakt/tilsetningsforordningen-endringsbestemmelser-om-bruk-av-stoffer-pa-eggeskall/id-5444 (2013).

Fagan, M. M. 'The Uses of Insect Galls', *The American Naturalist* 52 (1918), pp. 155–76.

Food and Agriculture Organization of the United Nations. 'FAO STATS: Live Animals', sourced in 2017 from http://www.fao.org/faostat/en/#data/QA

International Sericultural Commission (ISC), 'Statistics', sourced in 2017 from http://inserco.org/en/statistics

Koeppel, A. & Holland, C. 'Progress and Trends in Artificial Silk Spinning: A Systematic Review', *ACS Biomaterials Science & Engineering* 3 (2017), pp. 226–37, 10.1021/acsbiomaterials.6b00669.

Lovdata. 'Forskrift om endring i forskrift om tilsetningsstoffer til næringsmidler', sourced in 2017 from https://lovdata.no/dokument/LTI/forskrift/2013-05-21-510 (2013).

Oba, Y. 2014. 'Insect Bioluminescence in the Post-Molecular Biology Era', *Insect Molecular Biology and Ecology*, CRC Press (2013), pp. 94–120.

Osawa, K., Sasaki, T. & Meyer-Rochow, V. 'New Observations on the Biology of Keroplatus nipponicus Okada 1938 (Diptera; Mycetophiloidea; Keroplatidae), a Bioluminescent Fungivorous Insect', *Entomologie Heute* 26 (2014), pp. 139–49.

Ottesen, P. S. 'Om gallveps (Cynipidae) og jakten på det forsvunne blekk', *Insekt-nytt* 25 (2000).

Rutherford, A. 'Synthetic Biology and the Rise of the "Spider-goats"', sourced in 2017 from https://www.theguardian. com/science/2012/jan/14/synthetic-biology-spider-goat-genetics (2012).

Seneca the Elder, Latin text and translations, Seneca the Elder, *Excerpta Controversiae* 2.7, sourced in 2017 from http://perseus.uchicago.edu/perseus-cgi/citequery3. pl?dbname=LatinAugust2012&getid=0&query=Sen.%20 Con.%20ex.%202.7

Shah, T. H., Thomas, M. & Bhandari, R. 'Lac Production, Constraints and Management – a Review', *International Journal of Current Research* 7 (2015), pp. 13652–9.

Sutherland, T. D., Young, J. H., Weisman, S. et al. 'Insect Silk: One Name, Many Materials', *Annual Review of Entomology* 55 (2010), pp. 171–88.

Sveriges lantbruksuniversitet. 'Spinning Spider Silk Is Now Possible', sourced in 2017 from http://www.slu.se/en/ew-news/2017/1/spinning-spider-silk-is-now-possible/ (2017).

Tomasik, B. 'Insect Suffering from Silk, Shellac, Carmine, and Other Insect Products', sourced in 2017 from http:// reducing-suffering.org/insect-suffering-silk-shellac-carmine-insect-products/ (2017).

Wakeman, R. J., 2015. 'The Origin and Many Uses of Shellac', sourced in 2017 from https://www.antiquephono.org/the-origin-many-uses-of-shellac-by-r-j-wakeman/

Zinsser & Co. 'The Story of Shellac', sourced in 2017 from http:// www.zinsseruk.com/core/wp-content/uploads/2016/12/ Story-of-shellac.pdf, Somerseth, NJ (2003).

SOURCES

CHAPTER 8:
Life-savers, Pioneers and Nobel Prize-winners:
Insights from Insects

Aarnes, H. 'Biomimikry', sourced in 2017 from https://snl.no/ Biomimikry (2016).

Alnaimat, S. 'A Contribution to the Study of Biocontrol Agents, Apitherapy and Other Potential Alternative to Antibiotics', PhD thesis, University of Sheffield (2011).

Amdam, G. V. & Omholt, S. W. 'The Regulatory Anatomy of Honeybee Lifespan', *Journal of Theoretical Biology* 216 (2002), pp. 209–28.

Arup.com. 'Eastgate Development, Harare, Zimbabwe' sourced in 2017 from https://web.archive.org/web/20041 114141220/http://www.arup.com/feature.cfm?pageid=292

Bai, L., Xie, Z., Wang, W. et al. 'Bio-Inspired Vapor-Responsive Colloidal Photonic Crystal Patterns by Inkjet Printing', *ACS Nano* 8 (2014), 11094–100.

Baker, N., Wolschin, F. & Amdam, G. V. 'Age-Related Learning Deficits Can Be Reversible in Honeybees *Apis mellifera*', *Experimental Gerontology* 47 (2012), pp. 764–72.

BBC News. 'India Bank Termites Eat Piles of Cash', sourced in 2017 from http://www.bbc.com/news/world-south-asia-13194864 (2011).

Bombelli, P., Howe, C. J. & Bertocchini, F. 'Polyethylene Bio-degradation by Caterpillars of the Wax Moth *Galleria mellonella*', *Current Biology* 27: pp. R292–3 (2017).

Carville, O. 'The Great Tourism Squeeze: Small Town Tourist Destinations Buckle under Weight of New Zealand's Tourism Boom', sourced in 2017 from http://www.nzherald.co.nz/nz/news/article.cfm?c_id=1&objectid=11828398 (2017).

273

Chechetka, S. A., Yu, Y., Tange, M. & Miyako, E. 'Materially Engineered Artificial Pollinators', *Chem* 2: 224–39 (2017).

Christmann, B. 'Fly on the Wall. Making Fly Science Approachable for Everyone', sourced in 2017 from http://blogs.brandeis.edu/flyonthewall/list-of-posts/

Cornette, R. & Kikawada, T. 'The Induction of Anhydrobiosis in the Sleeping Chironomid: Current Status of our Knowledge', *IUBMB Life* 63 (2011), pp. 419–29.

Dirafzoon, A., Bozkurt, A. & Lobaton, E. 'A Framework for Mapping with Biobotic Insect Networks: From Local to Global Maps', *Robotics and Autonomous Systems* 88 (2017), pp. 79–96.

Doan, A. 'Biomimetic architecture: Green Building in Zimbabwe Modeled After Termite Mounds', sourced in 2017 from http://inhabitat.com/building-modelled-on-termites-eastgate-centre-in-zimbabwe/ (2012).

Drew, J. & Joseph, J. *The Story of the Fly: And How it Could Save the World*, Cheviot Publishing, Country Green Point, South Africa, 2012.

Dumanli, A. G. & Savin, T. 'Recent Advances in the Biomimicry of Structural Colours', *Chemical Society Reviews* 45 (2016), pp. 6698–724.

Fernández-Marín, H., Zimmerman, J. K., Rehner, S. A. & Wcislo, W. T. 'Active Use of the Metapleural Glands by Ants in Controlling Fungal Infection', *Proceedings of the Royal Society B: Biological Sciences* 273 (2006), pp. 1689–95.

Google Patenter. 'Infrared sensor systems and devices', sourced in 2017 from https://www.google.com/patents/US7547886

Haeder, S., Wirth, R., Herz, H. & Spiteller, D. 'Candicidin-Producing *Streptomyces* Support Leaf-Cutting Ants to

Protect Their Fungus Garden Against the Pathogenic Fungus Escovopsis', *Proceedings of the National Academy of Sciences,* 106 (2009), pp. 4742–6.

Hamedi, A., Farjadian, S. & Karami, M. R. 'Immunomodulatory Properties of Trehala Manna Decoction and its Isolated Carbohydrate Macromolecules', *Journal of Ethnopharmacology* 162 (2015), pp. 121–6.

Horikawa, D. D. 'Survival of Tardigrades in Extreme Environments: A Model Animal for Astrobiology', in Altenbach, A. V., Bernhard, J. M. & Seckbach, J. (red.), *Anoxia: Evidence for Eukaryote Survival and Paleontological Strategies.* Springer Netherlands, Dordrecht (2012), pp. 205–17.

Hölldobler, B. & Engel-Siegel, H. 'On the Metapleural Gland of Ants', *Psyche* 91 (1984), pp. 201–24.

King, H., Ocko, S. & Mahadevan, L. 'Termite Mounds Harness Diurnal Temperature Oscillations for Ventilation', *Proceedings of the National Academy of Sciences* 112 (2015), pp. 11589–93.

Ko, H. J., Youn, C. H., Kim, S. H. & Kim, S. Y. 'Effect of Pet Insects on the Psychological Health of Community-dwelling Elderly People: A Single-blinded, Randomized, Controlled Trial', *Gerontology* 62 (2016), pp. 200–9.

Kuo, F. E. & Sullivan, W. C. 'Environment and Crime in the Inner City: Does Vegetation Reduce Crime?' *Environment and Behavior* 33 (2001), pp. 343–67.

Kuo, M. 'How Might Contact with Nature Promote Human Health? Promising Mechanisms and a Possible Central Pathway', *Frontiers in Psychology* 6 (2015).

Liu, F., Dong, B. Q., Liu, X. H. et al. 'Structural Color Change in Longhorn Beetles *Tmesisternus isabellae*', *Optics Express* 17 (2009), pp. 16183–91.

McAlister, E. *The Secret Life of Flies*, Natural History Museum, London, 2017.

North Carolina State University. 'Tracking the Movement of Cyborg Cockroaches', sourced in 2017 from https://www.eurekalert.org/pub_releases/2017-02/ncsu-ttm022717.php (2017).

Novikova, N., Gusev, O., Polikarpov, N. et al. 'Survival of Dormant Organisms After Long-term Exposure to the Space Environment', *Acta Astronautica* 68 (2011), pp. 1574–80.

Pinar. 'Entire Alphabet Found on the Wing Patterns of Butterflies', sourced in 2017 from http://mymodernmet.com/kjell-bloch-sandved-butterfly-alphabet/ (2013).

Ramadhar, T. R., Beemelmanns, C., Currie, C. R. & Clardy, J. 'Bacterial Symbionts in Agricultural Systems Provide a Strategic Source for Antibiotic Discovery', *The Journal of Antibiotics* 67 (2014), pp. 53–8.

Rance, C. 'A Breath of Maggoty Air', sourced in 2017 from http://thequackdoctor.com/index.php/a-breath-of-maggoty-air/ (2016).

Sleeping Chironomid Research Group. 'About the Sleeping Chironomid', sourced in 2017 from http://www.naro.affrc.go.jp/archive/nias/anhydrobiosis/Sleeping%20Chironimid/e-about-yusurika.html

Sogame, Y. & Kikawada, T. 'Current Findings on the Molecular Mechanisms Underlying Anhydrobiosis in *Polypedilum vanderplanki*', *Current Opinion in Insect Science* 19 (2017), pp. 16–21.

Sowards, L. A., Schmitz, H., Tomlin, D. W. et al. 'Characterization of Beetle *Melanophila acuminata* (Coleoptera: Buprestidae) Infrared Pit Organs by High-Performance Liquid Chromatography/Mass Spectrometry, Scanning Electron

Microscope, and Fourier Transform-Infrared Spectroscopy', *Annals of the Entomological Society of America* 94 (2001), pp. 686–94.

Van Arnam, E. B., Ruzzini, A. C., Sit, C. S. et al. 'Selvamicin, an Atypical Antifungal Polyene from Two Alternative Genomic Contexts', *Proceedings of the National Academy of Sciences of the United States of America* 113 (2016), pp. 12940–45.

Wainwright, M., Laswd, A. & Alharbi, S. 'When Maggot Fumes Cured Tuberculosis', *Microbiologist* March 2007 (2007), pp. 33–5.

Watanabe, M. 'Anhydrobiosis in Invertebrates', *Applied Entomology and Zoology* 41 (2006), pp. 15–31.

Whitaker, I. S., Twine, C., Whitaker, M. J. et al. 'Larval Therapy from Antiquity to the Present Day: Mechanisms of Action, Clinical Applications and Future Potential', *Postgraduate Medical Journal* 83 (2007), pp. 409–13.

Wilson, E. O. *Biophilia*, Harvard University Press, Cambridge, Mass, 1984.

World Economic Forum, Ellen MacArthur Foundation and McKinsey & Company. 2016. 'The New Plastics Economy Rethinking the Future of Plastics', sourced in 2017 from https://www.ellenmacarthurfoundation.org/assets/downloads/EllenMacArthurFoundation_TheNewPlasticsEconomy_Pages.pdf

Yang, Y., Yang, J., Wu, W. M. et al. 'Biodegradation and Mineralization of Polystyrene by Plastic-Eating Mealworms: Part 1. Chemical and Physical Characterization and Isotopic Tests', *Environmental Science & Technology* 49 (2015), pp. 12080–86.

Yates, D. (2009). 'The Science Suggests Access to Nature Is Essential to Human Health', sourced in 2017 from https://news.illinois.edu/blog/view/6367/206035

Wodsedalek, J. E. 'Five Years of Starvation of Larvae', *Science* 1189 (1917), pp. 366–7, http://science.sciencemag.org/content/46/1189/366

Zhang, C.-X., Tang, X.-D. & Cheng, J.-A. 'The Utilization and Industrialization of Insect Resources in China', *Entomological Research* 38 (2008), pp. S38–S47.

CHAPTER 9:
Insects and Us: What's Next? and Afterword

Brandt, A., Gorenflo, A., Siede, R. et al. 'The Neonicotinoids Thiacloprid, Imidacloprid, and Clothianidin Affect the Immunocompetence of Honeybees (*Apis mellifera* L.)', *Journal of Insect Physiology* 86 (2016), pp. 40–7.

Byrne, K. & Nichols, R. A. '*Culex pipiens* in London Underground Tunnels: Differentiation Between Surface and Subterranean Populations', *Heredity* 82 (1999), 7–15.

Dirzo, R., Young, H. S., Galetti, M. et al. 'Defaunation in the Anthropocene', *Science* 345 (2014), pp. 401–6.

Dumbacher, J. P., Wako, A., Derrickson, S. R. et al. 'Melyrid Beetles (*Choresine*): A Putative Source for the Batrachotoxin Alkaloids Found in Poison-Dart Frogs and Toxic Passerine Birds', *Proceedings of the National Academy of Sciences of the United States of America* 101 (2004), pp. 15857–60.

Follestad, A. 'Effekter av kunstig nattbelysning på naturmangfoldet – en litteraturstudie', *NINA Rapport* 1081. 89 pages (2014).

Forbes, A. A., Powell, T. H. Q., Stelinski, L. L. et al. 'Sequential Sympatric Speciation across Trophic Levels', *Science* 323 (2009), pp. 776–9.

Garibaldi, L. A., Steffan-Dewenter, I., Winfree, R. et al. 'Wild

Pollinators Enhance Fruit Set of Crops Regardless of Honeybee Abundance', *Science* 339 (2013), pp. 1608–11.

Gough, L. A., Sverdrup-Thygeson, A., Milberg, P. et al. 'Specialists in Ancient Trees Are More Affected by Climate than Generalists', *Ecology and Evolution* 5 (2015), pp. 5632–41.

Goulson, D. 'Review: An Overview of the Environmental Risks Posed by Neonicotinoid Insecticides', *Journal of Applied Ecology* 50 (2013), pp. 977–87.

Hallmann, C. A., Sorg, M., Jongejans, E. et al. 'More Than 75 Per Cent Decline Over 27 Years in Total Flying Insect Biomass in Protected Areas', *PLOS ONE* 12 (2017), e0185809.

IPBES. 'Summary for Policymakers of the Assessment Report of the Intergovernmental Science-Policy Platform on Biodiversity and Ecosystem Services on Pollinators, Pollination and Food Production', Secretariat of the Intergovernmental Science-Policy Platform on Biodiversity and Ecosystem Services, Bonn, Germany (2016).

McKinney, M. L. 'High Rates of Extinction and Threat in Poorly Studied Taxa', *Conservation Biology* 13 (1999), pp. 1273–81.

Morales, C., Montalva, J., Arbetman, M. et al. 2016. '*Bombus dahlbomii*. The IUCN Red List of Threatened Species 2016: e.T21215142A100240441', sourced in 2017 from http://dx.doi.org/10.2305/IUCN.UK.2016-3.RLTS.T21215142A100240441.en

Myers, C. W., Daly, J. W. & Malkin, B. 'A Dangerously Toxic New Frog (*Phyllobates*) Used by Embera Indians of Western Colombia with Discussion of Blowgun Fabrication and Dart Poisoning', *Bulletin of the American Museum of Natural History* 161 (1978), pp. 307–66.

Pawson, S. M. & Bader, M. K. F. 'LED Lighting Increases the

Ecological Impact of Light Pollution Irrespective of Color Temperature', *Ecological Applications* 24 (2014), pp. 1561–8.

Rader, R., Bartomeus, I., Garibaldi, L. A. et al. 'Non-Bee Insects Are Important Contributors to Global Crop Pollination', *Proceedings of the National Academy of Sciences* 113 (2016), pp. 146–51.

Rasmont, P., Franzén, M., Lecocq, T. et al. 'Climatic Risk and Distribution Atlas of European Bumblebees', *BioRisk* 10 (2015).

Säterberg, T., Sellman, S. & Ebenman, B. 'High Frequency of Functional Extinctions in Ecological Networks', *Nature* 499 (2013), pp. 468–70.

Schwägerl, C. 'Vanishing Act. What's Causing the Sharp Decline in Insects, and Why It Matters', sourced in 2017 from https://e360.yale.edu/features/insect_numbers_declining_why_it_matters (2017).

Thoresen, S. B. 'Gendrivere – magisk medisin eller villfaren vitenskap?' sourced in 2017 from http://www.bioteknologiradet.no/2016/06/gen-drivere-magisk-medisin-eller-villfaren-vitenskap/ (2016).

Thoresen, S. B. & Rogne, S. 'Vi kan nå genmodifisere mygg så vi kanskje kvitter oss med malaria for godt', sourced in 2017 from https://www.aftenposten.no/viten/i/4m9o/Vi-kan-na-genmodifisere-mygg-sa-vi-kanskje-kvitter-oss-med-malaria-for-godt (2015).

Tsvetkov, N., Samson-Robert, O., Sood, K. et al. 'Chronic Exposure to Neonicotinoids Reduces Honeybee Health near Corn Crops', *Science* 356 (2017), p. 1395.

Vindstad, O. P. L., Schultze, S., Jepsen, J. U. et al. 'Numerical Responses of Saproxylic Beetles to Rapid Increases in Dead Wood Availability following Geometrid Moth

Outbreaks in Sub-Arctic Mountain Birch Forest', *PLOS ONE* 9 (2014).

Vogel, G. 'Where Have All the Insects Gone?' sourced in 2017 from http://www.sciencemag.org/news/2017/05/where-have-all-insects-gone (2017).

Wiggins, Glenn B. (1927–2013). http://www.zobodat.at/biografien/Wiggins_Glenn_B_BRA_42_0004-0008.pdf

Wilson, E. O. 'The Little Things That Run the world (The Importance and Conservation of Invertebrates)', *Conservation Biology* 1 (1987), pp. 344–6.

Woodcock, B. A., Bullock, J. M., Shore, R. F. et al. 'Country-specific Effects of Neonicotinoid Pesticides on Honeybees and Wild Bees', *Science* 356 (2017), p. 1393.

Zeuss, D., Brandl, R., Brändle, M. et al. 'Global Warming Favours Light-coloured Insects in Europe', *Nature Communications* 5 (2014), Article No. 3874.

Index